D0897750

AFRICAN HISTORICAL DICTIONARIES
Edited by Jon Woronoff

HISTORICAL DICTIONARY OF THE COMORO ISLANDS

by
Martin Ottenheimer
and
Harriet Ottenheimer

African Historical Dictionaries No. 59

The Scarecrow Press, Inc.
Metuchen, N.J., & London
1994

OBN 1276387

REF
DT
469
.C7
O88
1994

British Library Cataloguing-in-Publication data available

Library of Congress Cataloging-in-Publication Data

Ottenheimer, Martin
    Historical dictionary of the Comoro Islands / by Martin
Ottenheimer and Harriet Ottenheimer
       p. cm. — (African historical dictionaries ; no.59)
    Includes bibliographical references.
    ISBN 0-8108-2819-7 (alk. paper)
    1. Comoros—History—Dictionaries. I. Ottenheimer,
Harriet, 1941– . II. Title. III. Series.
DT469.C7088   1994
969.4′003—dc20   93-42244

CONTENTS

EDITOR'S FOREWORD

Relatively small in size and small in population, located off the east coast of Africa and still divided in many ways, the Comoro Islands have long been outside the mainstream of African affairs. This relative isolation has allowed them to develop unique economic, social, and cultural features that deserve to be better known, as does their unusual political position. As time passes, the Comoros will gradually enter the mainstream, a process that began already with independence. This is yet another reason to become more familiar with the Comoros and the Comorians.

Even those who have wanted to know more have been stymied by a lack of information. This gap is now filled in good part by the latest African Historical Dictionary. It takes a very close, careful, and caring look at the Comoro Islands. It traces an intriguing history to the present. It shows the main social and cultural features. And it assesses the economic and political prospects. Another contribution, of equal significance, is the comprehensive bibliography that points readers who wish to learn yet more in the right directions.

This volume was written by two leading authorities, the impressive team of Martin and Harriet Ottenheimer. Both teach anthropology at Kansas State University, where he is past head of the Department of Sociology, Anthropology, and Social Work, and she is director of American Ethnic Studies. They have visited and done research in the Comoros regularly and also written articles, reviews, and books. Among them are *Marriage in Domoni* by Martin, a *ShiNzwani-English Dictionary* by Harriet and *Music of the Comoro Islands—Domoni* by both Ottenheimers.

Jon Woronoff
Series Editor

ACKNOWLEDGMENTS

Special thanks to Sophy Blanchy, Damir Ben Ali, Jean Gorse, Tom Hinnebusch, Charles Kisseberth, Françoise LeGuinnec Coppens, Michel Lafon, Michael Lambek, Tom McCoid, Derek Nurse, Bob Smith, Souifaoui Affane, Pierre Vérin, and Henry Wright who provided copies of articles and references to help make the bibliography the most complete and accurate one ever published on the Comoro Islands. We would also like to thank Afan and Davi Ottenheimer for contributing to the fieldwork and providing insight into the culture of the children of the Islands. This book has been made possible by many people, especially those in the Comoro Islands. Their cooperation was invaluable and their friendship cherished. While we cannot list them all there is one person who, because of his untiring efforts for education in the Islands and his determination to make the rest of the world aware of the place of the Comoro Islands in world history, stands out in our minds as an especially valuable friend and colleague. It is to the memory of Affane Mohamed that this book is dedicated.

NOTE ON SPELLING AND NAMES

There is currently a lack of agreement regarding the proper spelling of Comorian words and names. Different languages such as French, Arabic, and Swahili have all had their influence on Comorian spelling styles. Comorian was first written (and continues to be written) in Arabic script. With French colonization, French orthography was added and, as French schooling became common, French spellings also became common. During the Ali Soilih government of the mid-1970s French spellings were replaced with more phonemic-style spellings, in emulation of Swahili. A recent orthographic study conducted in the Comoros has proposed a modified phonemic spelling which attempts to take inter-island variations into account. As a result of this history, and of the fact that no clear standard has yet emerged for the spelling of Comorian, words and names are frequently spelled two or more different ways. The compromise we have adopted for this volume follows common Comorian usage: French spellings for most names of people and places (especially as most maps still use these old spellings), and phonemic spellings for names of islands, large towns, and common words.

In the case of Mahoré, the authors have used the older French spelling rather than the newer Comorian spelling of Maore in recognition of the fact that the island has remained associated with France rather than joining with the other three islands in independence.

Following Islamic tradition, most Comorian men's names consist of two parts: a given name followed by one's father's name (patronymic); occasionally a grandfather's name is also added. In referring to an individual, one uses the given name alone or the given plus the patronymic names together. The patronymic is never used alone, as a last name, and would be misleading.

CHRONOLOGY

c. 650   The date of the introduction of Islam to the Comoros according to local traditions.

c. 900   Earliest archaeological evidence for widespread occupation of the Comoro Islands.

c. 1200   Suggested date for the arrival of the Shirazi migrants, traditional ancestral population for several different groups of people in the Comoros and on the East African coast.

c. 1500   The Portuguese soon after their first presence in the Indian Ocean visit the islands.

1591   Thirty-five men under James Lancaster sailing on the English vessel *Edward Bonaventure* are massacred on Ngazidja.

1607   After their unsuccessful attack against the Portuguese at Mozambique Island, the Dutch retreat to the island of Mahoré and buy supplies to refurbish their fleet.

c. 1685   Establishment on the islands of the lineage of Abu Bakr b. Salim, Muslim saint from Hadramawt in Southern Arabia.

1693   The pirates Mission and Caraccioli arrive at Nzwani and offer their services to Queen Halima I.

1793   The beginning of the Malagasy incursions to the islands.

1841   The Malagasy ruler of Mahoré cedes the island to France.

1885   The French naturalist, Léon Humblot, arrives in the Comoro Islands and sets up base on Ngazidja. A treaty is signed that puts Ngazidja under French protectorship.

1886   The islands of Nzwani and Mwali become French protectorates.

1889	The administrative unity of Mahoré with the other islands is decreed by France.
1891	A rebellion of slaves in Nzwani results in the sacking of the ancient capital of the island, Domoni, and the presence of French troops on the island.
1896	Comoros administratively attached to Réunion.
1908	The Comoros are administratively attached to Madagascar.
1909	Nzwani is officially abdicated to France by the Sultan of the island.
1912	The islands are declared by France to be colonies.
1946	The Comoros become an Overseas Territory of France with representation in the French National Assembly but remain under the authority of the High Commissioner of Madagascar.
1952	The Coelacanth, a fish thought to have been extinct for 70 million years, is caught off the island of Nzwani and brought to the attention of western scientists.
1958	The capital of the territory is moved from Dzaoudzi, Mahoré, to Moroni, Ngazidja.
1961	The Comoro Islands are granted administrative autonomy. An elected Territorial Legislature (Chamber of Deputies of the Comoros) and a Government Council with a President and Ministers are established. The President of the Council is recognized as President of the territory. Government is under a French High Commissioner who reports to the Minister of Overseas Territories and Departments. Saïd Mohamed Cheikh, the President of the Government Council, becomes the first territorial President of the Comoros.
1962	Mouvement pour la liberation national des Comores (MOLINACO) is formed (National Liberation Movement of the Comoros).
1968	Formation of political party, Rassemblement démocratique des peuples Comoriens (RDPC), the Democratic Assembly of the Comorian People. It later becomes known as the "white party" because its candidates are placed on white ballots during elections. Formation of another party, Union démocra-

tique des Comores (UDC), the Democratic Union of the Comoros. It later becomes known as the "green party" because of the green ballots used for its candidates in elections. The expulsion of the Comorian communities from Zanzibar and Pemba results in a number of migrants settling in the islands. Rioting of Lycée students in Moroni results from growing tension between the French and Comorians.

1969   Formation of Parti socialiste des Comores (PASOCO), the Socialist Party of the Comoros.

1970   Death of the first territorial President of the Comoros, Saïd Mohamed Cheikh; Prince Saïd Ibrahim becomes territorial President.

1971   Formation of UMMA (The People). The party advocates independence only with France's consent and comes under the control of the future leader of the Comoros, Ali Soilih.

1972   Formation of Parti pour l'évolution des Comores (PEC), the Party for the Evolution of the Comoros; Prince Saïd Mohammed Djaffar becomes President of the council of government and publicly demands independence from France; he then resigns, precipitating an election in which Ahmed Abdallah, leader of the UDC party, becomes President of the council of government.

1973   The UDC and RDPC parties merge to form the Parti pour l'indépendance et l'unité des Comores (PUIC), Party for Independence and Unity in the Comoros.

1974   Referendum on independence with Mahoré voting not to become independent, while the other three islands vote overwhelmingly for independence from France.

1975   The declaration of independence of the Comoro Islands is made on July 6th. Ahmed Abdallah is elected chief of state and deposed by a coup led by Ali Soilih the following month. Saïd Mohammed Djaffar is chosen as interim President. France recognizes the independence of Ngazidja, Nzwani, and Mwali but calls for a referendum on Mahoré. The Comoro Islands are admitted to the United Nations.

1976   Ali Soilih becomes President. People in Mahoré vote overwhelmingly in a referendum to remain separate from the independent Comoro Islands and stay with France. The island is retained by France as a "collectivité territoriale."

1977   Survivors of massacres in Madagascar, particularly in the city of Majunga, arrive in the islands. The Comoros under Ali Soilih are proclaimed to be a democratic, secular, socialist republic.

1978   Mercenaries under the leadership of Robert Denard overthrow the government and kill Ali Soilih. Ahmed Abdallah and Mohamed Ahmed are installed as Co-presidents and then Ahmed Abdallah is elected as sole President for a six-year term. A new constitution, recognizing Islam as the national religion and creating a federal Islamic republic, is approved by popular referendum. Comoros are expelled from a conference of the OAU because of the mercenary presence.

1979   The newly established Federal Assembly votes to establish a one-party system until 1991.

1984   Founding of Union pour une République Démocratique aux Comores (UPRD), the Union for a Democratic Republic in the Comoros, in Paris by Abdallah Mouazoir, Ali Soilih's former foreign minister. Ahmed Abdallah is re-elected President.

1985   Leader of the UPRD, Moustapha Saïd Cheikh, is incriminated in a plot to overthrow the President. He and 53 party members are jailed. The Comoros are admitted to the Indian Ocean Commission, a regional organization dedicated to the promotion of co-operation and economic development, joining Madagascar, the Seychelles, and Mauritius.

1987   The Comoro government concludes an agreement with South African authorities to construct and refurbish hotels for tourism.

1989   President Ahmed Abdallah is assassinated by the mercenaries on the Comoros under Robert Denard. Saïd Mohamed Djohar, Chief Justice of the Supreme Court, and half-brother of Ali Soilih, is named interim President. France brings troops to the islands and forces the mercenaries to leave the Comoros. Denard moves to South Africa.

1990   General amnesty is granted to all political prisoners. Saïd Mohamed Djohar is elected President in two elections after the first one is abandoned due to claims of fraud by his opponent Mohamed Taki. An attempted coup fails to oust President Djohar. A multiparty system is reinstated. Formation of the political party Mouvement pour la rénovation et l'action démocratique (MOURAD), Movement for Renovation and Democratic Action. The UPRD party is reorganized and renamed "Uwezo" (leadership). Formal diplomatic relations with the United States are established. President Mitterand of France pays a one-day official visit to the islands. South Africa and the Comoros sign a bilateral agreement for Comorian development.

1991   The Chief Justice of the Supreme Court is arrested after being accused of leading an attempted coup. Formation of the political party Rassemblement pour le changement et la démocratie (RACHADE), Assembly for Change and Democracy.

1994   Several opposition leaders are arrested in Moroni following a failed assassination attempt on President Saïd Mohamed Djohar.

ABBREVIATIONS

ACCT	Agence de Coopération Culturelle et Technique
ASEC	Association des Stagiaires et Étudiants Comoriens
ASEMI	Asie du Sud-Est et Monde Insulindien
CEROI	Le Centre d'Études et de Recherche sur l'Ocèan Indien
CFA	Central African Franc
CHEAM	Centre des Hautes Études Administratives sur l'Afrique et l'Asie Modernes
CHUMA	Fraternity and Unity Party
CILF	Conseil International de la Langue Française
CNDRS	Centre National de Documentation et de Recherche Scientifique
EEDC	Électricité et Eaux des Comores
FAO	Food and Agriculture Organization of the United Nations
FD	Front Démocratique
FIDES	Fonds de Développement Économique et Social
FNUC	Front National pour la Unification des Comores
FNUK	Front National uni des Komores; see also FNUC
INALCO	Institut National des Langues et Civilisations Orientales
MDP	Mouvement Démocratique Populaire
MOLINACO	Mouvement pour la Libération National des Comores
MOURAD	Mouvement pour la Rénovation et l'Action Démocratique
OAU	Organization of African Unity
ORSTOM	Office de la Recherche Scientifique et Technique Outre-Mer
PASOCO	Parti Socialiste des Comores

PCDP   Parti Comorien pour la Démocratie et le Progrès
PEC   Parti pour l'Évolution des Comores
PSDC   Parti Social Démocratique des Comores
PUIC   Parti pour l'Indépendance et l'Unité des Comores
RACHADE   Rassemblement pour le Changement et la Démocratie
RDPC   Rassemblement Démocratique des Peuples Comoriens
RENAMO   Resistencia Nacional Moçambicana
SAGC   Société Anonyme de la Grande Comore
SCB   Société Colonial de Bambao
SELAF   Société d'Études Linguistiques et Anthropologiques de France
SODEC   Société pour le Développement Economique des Comores
TOM   Territoire d'Outre-Mer
UCP   Union Comorienne pour le Progrès
UDC   Union Démocratique des Comores
UDZIMA   Union Comorienne pour le Progrès; see also UCP
UMMA   The People
UNDC   Union Nationale pour la Démocratie aux Comores
URDC   Union pour une République Démocratique aux Comores
UWEZO   See URDC

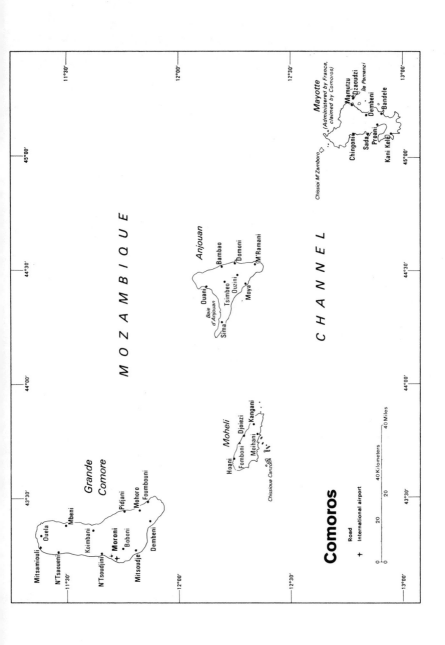

Comoros

Road
+ International airport

0   20   40 Kilometers
0   20   40 Miles

Grande Comore

Mitsamiouli
N'Tsaoueni
Ouela
Mbeni
Koimbani
N'Tsoudjini
Moroni +
Boboni
Mitsoudje
Pidjani
Mohoro
Foumbouni
Dembeni

MOZAMBIQUE

Moheli

Hoani
Fomboni
Moihani
Djoiezi
Kangani

Chissioua Canzoni

Anjouan

Baie d'Anjouan
Ouani
Sima
Tsimbeo
Ouzini
Bambao
Domoni
Moya
M'Ramani

CHANNEL

Chissioi M'Zamboro

Mayotte
(Administered by France,
claimed by Comoros)

Chingoni
Mamutzu
Tzaoudzi
Ile Pamanzi
Sada
Proani
Dembeni
Bandele
Kani Kele

INTRODUCTION
THE COMOROS, AN OVERVIEW

GEOGRAPHY

The Comoro Islands are an archipelago of four islands and several islets located halfway between the island of Madagascar and eastern Africa at the northern end of the Mozambique Channel. The total area of the four islands is 863 square miles (2,236 square kilometers). They lie along a northwest-southeast axis within sight of each other but are quite distinct.

Ngazidja (formerly called Grande Comore) is the largest of the islands and youngest in geologic age. It is dominated by an active volcano, Karthala, that rises to a height of 9,186 feet (2,800 meters), and its landscape is marked by jagged rocks of lava and the absence of any streams or rivers. The capital, major seaport, and largest town of the islands, Moroni, lies on its western shore.

Southeast of Ngazidja is Mwali (formerly called Mohéli), the smallest of the four islands. It is a fertile island with a central mountain range rising 2,556 feet (790 meters) above sea level. The chief town, Fomboni, is located on its northern shore.

East of Mwali is Nzwani (formerly called Anjouan), the most densely populated of the islands. Its central peak rises 5,072 feet (1,575 meters) above sea level. With its black, sandy beaches, fast-moving streams, and (now disappearing) luxurious tropical forest, it is often referred to as the "Pearl of the Indian Ocean." The largest town is Mutsamudu, located on a northwestern bay of the island. The bay was a stopover for many European sailing ships during the eighteenth and nineteenth centuries, and today the town is the second most important port in the islands.

The most easterly of the islands and the closest to Madagascar, Mahoré (formerly called Mayotte), is geologically the oldest. It is the most eroded and consequently the lowest of the islands with slow meandering streams and mangrove swamps. There is also an extensive coral reef. Its chief town, Dzaoudzi, used to be the French administrative capital of the archipelago. It is a port located on the islet of Pamandzi off the east coast of Mahoré. The island remains under French administration.

CLIMATE

The Comoros' location between 11 and 13 degrees south of the equator in the western Indian Ocean places them in a maritime tropical climate. In the wet season from October to April, the predominant northerly winds of the Indian Ocean bring moist, warm air to the region. Heaviest rainfall occurs during the period from December to April and amounts can reach as high as 15 inches (390 mm) in a month. The mean temperature during the wet season is in the high seventies (75–79°F; 24–26°C) with the hottest month, March, averaging temperatures in the middle eighties (84–86°F; 29–30°C). From May to September southerly winds due to high pressure centers in southern Africa dominate the region. These cooler, drier winds drop temperatures to an average low of 66°F (19°C). Rainfall and temperature varies from island to island during any month and even on parts of an island due to topographical variation. The central, higher areas of Nzwani, for example, are often cooler and moister than the coastal areas. Its central peak, Ntingui, is often shrouded in mist.

POPULATION

The islands are one of the most densely populated areas of Africa. The total population in 1991 was estimated to be 476,678, with over 27% living in urban areas. The 1980 census reported the average density to be 182.5 persons per square kilometer, varying between 65.5 persons per square kilometer in Mwali and 349.1 persons per square kilometer in Nzwani. In recent decades the population was augmented by the forced evacuation of people of Comoro Island descent from Madagascar and Zanzibar and their resettlement in the Comoros. The present population increase is an estimated 3.5% per year with an annual birth rate of

47 births per 1,000 and an annual death rate of 12 deaths per 1,000 population. The most recent estimate of the total fertility rate is 6.8 children born per woman. Life expectancy at birth is 54 years for males and 59 years for females. The inhabitants are a blend of various peoples of the Indian Ocean littoral with African, Malagasy, and Arabic features strongly evident. Involved in maritime commerce before the appearance of Europeans in the Indian Ocean at the end of the fifteenth century, islanders had contacts with peoples from southern Africa to southeast Asia. More recent influences can be traced to European presence in the islands, especially since the middle of the nineteenth century when France became the dominant external influence on the archipelago. Outside of the island of Mahoré, where there are a number of Christians, islanders are predominantly Sunni Muslims conforming to the Shafii rite.

LANGUAGE

The official languages of the islands are French and Arabic with the former used primarily in politics and business, the latter in religion. Most people speak one or more varieties of Comorian, the language group indigenous to the islands. Closely related to the Swahili of the East African coast, Comorian is typical of most Bantu languages, with a large number of noun classes and an elaborate set of verb tenses and aspects. The rich vocabulary of Comorian has been enhanced by the borrowing of words from many other languages through centuries of external contact and trade. There are four varieties, ShiNgazidja, ShiMwali, ShiNzwani, and ShiMahoré, each one named for the island on which it is spoken.

ECONOMY

Agriculture is the principal economic activity with crops grown both for domestic consumption and export. The major food crops are cassava, coconut, bananas, rice, sweet potatoes, pulses, and corn. Vanilla, ylang-ylang, cloves, and copra have been the major export crops. The Comoros are the world's leading producer of the essence of ylang-ylang, widely used in the perfume industry, and are the world's second-largest producer of vanilla. Animal husbandry is maintained on a small scale with sheep, goats, and cattle kept by individual farmers. Some fishing is done but in spite of aid from Japan and cooperative agreements with European countries the industry remains on a very small scale. Some income has been generated by the catching and sale of Coelacanth specimens. This fish, thought to have been extinct for more than 70 million years, has been caught in Comorian waters and sold to museums and research centers all over the world. Tourism has been promoted to a degree, and South African commercial interests have recently been developing an infrastructure and promoting tourism in the islands.

Due mostly to overpopulation much foodstuff is now imported. Most of the meat, vegetables, and rice consumed are brought in; with the additional import of petroleum products, equipment, and construction materials, the islands have had a negative balance of trade for some time. Imports of goods and services in 1989 amounted to $77,940,000, while exports were only $39,640,000. The government has sought external aid, and a number of countries and private voluntary organizations have provided it. France is the Comoro Islands' principal trading partner. Until the end of 1993 the Comorian franc was tied to the French franc at an exchange rate of fifty to one (50 CF = 1 FF).

RECENT HISTORY

At the Berlin conference in 1885–86 France, Great Britain, and Germany came to an agreement under which France would be left alone to exercise control over the Comoro Islands and Madagascar. France already had control over the island of Mahoré—it had been established as a French protectorate in 1843—and by 1909, with the previous agreement of the other major European colonial powers, France made the other three islands protectorates as well. In 1912 the Comoros were declared to be a colony of France and attached administratively to Madagascar.

At the end of World War II, the islands were given financial and administrative autonomy and representation in the French legislature but still remained under the authority of a High Commissioner in Madagascar. Complete administrative autonomy was granted to the islands in 1961, and a domestic government was established. This consisted of an elected Chamber of Deputies who selected a Government Council headed by a President. The President of the Council was the territory's local head of government. The President and the remainder of the Comorian government still remained under a French High Commissioner, however. But, whereas the High Commissioner concerned with the governing of the islands previously was located in Madagascar, the Commissioner now resided in the islands.

In the late 1960s and continuing through the early 1970s pressures grew in the Comoros for independence from France. In 1973 the French signed an agreement that would give independence to the Comoro Islands subject to a referendum to be held within five years. At the same time Ahmed Abdallah, then the President of the Government Council, was declared to be President of the Comoros. The role of the French High Commissioner in internal affairs was effectively eliminated, but France retained control of foreign affairs, defense, and matters of currency. The following year a referendum was held, and an overwhelming majority of votes were cast in favor of independence. Only in Mahoré was there a majority vote against it. It was clear that a large number of people on the island of Mahoré preferred to remain under French control rather than join an independent unit essentially controlled by the other islands. In 1975, when the French parliament decided that any constitutional proposals of an independent Comoro Islands were to be ratified on an island-by-island basis, the Chamber of Deputies approved a unilateral declaration of independence, and Ahmed Abdallah was elected the President of the independent country. France did nothing to stop this move. In November 1975, the United Nations admitted the new country, including Mahoré, while France recognized the independence of three of the islands but retained control of Mahoré. Relations between France and the independent Comoros were then suspended.

Shortly after the declaration of independence a coup took place that deposed Ahmed Abdallah as President; Ali Soilih was installed as President in January 1976. Under Ali Soilih's government the Comoros were declared to be a democratic, secular, socialist republic and underwent a period of turmoil in which records were destroyed, the civil service dismantled, land was redistributed, local government replaced, and strong opposition to religion was espoused. This ended in May 1978, when a group of mercenaries led by Robert Denard overthrew the government and imprisoned Soilih, who was soon killed "while trying to escape." The islands held a referendum approving a new constitution in which the country was established as a federal Islamic republic, and Ahmed Abdallah was elected President for a term of six years. The new constitution allowed for a degree of autonomy for each island under a governor and provided each island with representation in a federal assembly. The status of the island of Mahoré was left to be decided at a later date. France resumed relations with the islands and again provided economic and technical assistance. Other countries, including South Africa, also provide assistance.

In November 1989, President Ahmed Abdallah was assassinated by mercenaries. Saïd Mohamed Djohar, Chief Justice of the Supreme Court, was constitutionally mandated to replace the President until an election could be held, but he was replaced as head of state by the mercenaries who attempted to directly seize power. France and South Africa then suspended their aid, and France landed military personnel to forcibly expel the mercenaries from the islands. In 1990 Saïd Mohamed Djohar was elected to the presidency in two elections; the second was held after allegations of fraudulent voting in the first one. President Mitterrand of France visited the islands, and France resumed its aid. It was also agreed that a French military presence would remain on the islands for at least two years to train local security forces. The United States began formal relations with the country, and South Africa resumed relations with the islands providing aid as well as loans to support development in the Comoros.

Some political unrest continues today in the Comoros because of the disputed status of Mahoré. The precariousness of the economy and traditional animosities are other features of the present social landscape that contribute to continuing political turbulence. In 1991, the lengthy political turmoil in the islands continued with the arrest of the President of the Supreme Court for allegedly leading a failed coup against President Djohar.

POLITICAL ORGANIZATION

The three islands of Ngazidja, Nzwani, and Mwali are separate administrative divisions with governors and elected councils that together make up the Federal Islamic Republic of the Comoro Islands. There is a dispute over the island of Mahoré, which has remained separate as a French territory. The Republic's constitution was passed in 1978 and subsequently amended in 1982, 1985, and 1989. It recognizes the right of universal suffrage for all citizens over 18 years of age, a legal system based on both French and Muslim law, and the autonomy of the separate islands in matters not specifically designated to the federal branches of government. There are three branches of federal government: executive, legislative, and judicial. The executive branch is made up of an elected President and his appointed council of ministers. The President is head of state. The term of office for the President is six years, and a person may be elected to office no more than three terms. If the position is left vacant, the President of the Supreme Court will take over as head of state until an election can be held. The last presidential election was held in 1990. The legislative branch consists of a unicameral federal assembly of forty-two members elected every five years. The last election was held in 1992. The legislature enacts laws concerning health, external trade, federal taxation, defence, education, communications, transport, federal crime, and economics. The judicial branch acts independently of the legislative and executive powers. It consists of a supreme court composed of three members elected by each island's council, two members elected by the federal assembly, two members appointed by the President, and former Presidents of the Republic. There have been several political parties active since 1989: Chuma (Fraternity and Unity Party), Front Démocratique (FD), Mouvement Démocratique Populaire (MDP), Mouvement pour la Renovation et l'Action Démocratique (MOURAD), Parti Comorien pour la Démocratie et le Progrès (PCDP), Parti Socialiste des Comores (PASOCO), Rassemblement pour le Changement et la Démocratie (RACHADE), Union Comorienne pour le Progrès (UCP, or Udzima), Union Nationale pour la Démocratie aux Comores (UNDC), and Uwezo (the reorganized Union pour une république démocratique aux Comores).

EDUCATION

There are 257 primary schools with more than 1,900 teachers and 36 secondary schools with three dozen teachers located throughout the islands. Teaching staff are enhanced by volunteers from countries in Europe, Africa, Arabia, and North America. Primary education begins at six years of age and lasts for six years. Secondary education has a four-year period followed by a period of three years. Although education is compulsory, the literacy rate in French is estimated to be only 46%. Those students wishing to continue their education beyond the level of secondary education must attend institutions overseas. Students have enrolled in educational institutions in many countries of the world, including China, Russia, Canada, the United States, Germany, and France. The greater majority have attended institutions of higher learning in France.

COMMUNICATION AND TRANSPORTATION

Two newspapers, three radio stations, and one television station serve the public as communication media. Telephone and radio systems make rapid inter-island communication exchange possible as well as contact with the external world. Four airports serve the islands with the main international airport located on Ngazidja. Direct service is available between France and the Comoros as well as between Africa and the islands. A local airline carries cargo and passengers between islands and between the islands and East Africa. Small sailing vessels carry passengers and cargo between islands as well. There are approximately 562 miles (900 kilometers) of roads, of which one-third are paved. The remainder are surfaced with crushed stone or gravel.

THE DICTIONARY

-A-

ABDALLAH I, SULTAN. Ruler of Nzwani (q.v.) from 1792 to 1803. The vizier of Sultan Ahmed, he came to power as the result of the assassination of Cheikh Salim (q.v.), Sultan Ahmed's son. Known as Mwenye Fani, he took the name of Sultan Abdallah when he ascended to the sultanate. He built up the defensive citadel at Mutsamudu (q.v.) and transferred the capital of Nzwani from Domoni (q.v.) to Mutsamudu. Relatives of Cheikh Salim, vowing revenge, enlisted the aid of Malagasy mercenaries who attacked Mutsamudu and burned the neighboring town of Wani (q.v.). In 1801 he abdicated in favor of his granddaughter Halima II, but she died soon after and he became sultan again. In 1803 he traveled to Bombay where he offered to cede the Comoros to the British. On his way back to the Comoros he learned that he had been deposed by Sultan Alaoui I (q.v.). When he finally returned to the Comoros it was to Mahoré (q.v.), where he died several years later.

ABDALLAH II, SULTAN. The eldest son of Sultan Alaoui I (q.v.), Abdallah II was the Sultan of Nzwani (q.v.) between 1823 and 1836. Having lived for a time in Mauritius, he spoke English, and he agreed to assist the British in their efforts to combat the slave trade. In 1826 Abdallah II provided asylum for Ramanataka (q.v.), the Merina general who had assisted in the conquering of the Sakalava coast in Madagascar but who found himself out of favor with the new Malagasy government. Abdallah II provided Ramanataka with land for himself and his soldiers in Nzwani and, in 1828, relied on his forces to establish control over Mwali (q.v.). In 1832 Abdallah II was dethroned by his younger brother (also with the aid of Ramanataka). He regained power in 1836 but died soon after.

ABDALLAH III, SULTAN. Ruler of the island of Nzwani (q.v.) during the last half of the nineteenth century, from 1855 until his death in 1891. Sultan Abdallah III signed a treaty with the French on April 21, 1886, accepting a French protectorate over the island. Although he signed a proclamation abolishing slavery in 1889, slavery was not effectively ended until shortly after his death.

ABDALLAH MOUAZOIR. A foreign minister in Ali Soilih's (q.v.) government, Abdallah Mouazoir was imprisoned by the Ahmed Abdallah (q.v.) government from 1982 to 1984. In 1984 he was exiled to Paris where he founded the Union pour une république démocratique aux Comores (q.v.). He returned to the Comoros in 1985 and attempted, unsuccessfully, to contest the elections in Ngazidja (q.v.).

AFFANE MOHAMED. A Governor of Nzwani (q.v.) in the 1980s, and a native of Domoni (q.v.), he was the first Comorian to teach French on the islands. He was also responsible for having brought the Coelacanth (q.v.) to the attention of J. P. Smith in South Africa (q.v.).

AGRICULTURE. Agriculture contributes approximately 41% of the gross domestic product in the Comoros. In addition to farming (cash and subsistence crops), this includes forestry, husbandry and fishing. Food crops account for 29% of agricultural production of which four-fifths are consumed locally. It is usually necessary to supplement locally grown foods with imports (q.v.), particularly in the case of rice. A 1981 yield of 156 pounds of rice per person, for example, provided only 10% of the total rice consumed in the islands that year. Oil, meat, and milk are other items for which local production does not meet demand; approximately 60 to 70% of these items are imported. In addition, wheat-flour and sugar have become part of the modern Comorian diet and 100% of these items must be imported. Overall, 42% of the foodstuffs consumed are imported. The islands produce

100% of their needs in chicken, eggs, corn, legumes, bananas, breadfruit, fresh vegetables, coconut (q.v.), and man-
ioc and other root crops, while nearly 90% of the fish (q.v.)
consumed is caught locally. Cash crops, which make up
12% of the GDP (1981), provide significant—though often
unpredictable—income. Chief among cash crops are vanilla
(q.v.), cloves (q.v.), and ylang-ylang (q.v.). Most farmers attempt to balance their output between food crops and cash
crops, but this is not always possible in every locality. In
general, cash crops, such as bananas and coconuts (q.v.), are
grown in the coastal areas, up to about 1600 feet of altitude,
while livestock and other food crops are produced on higher
land. Scarcity of land is another factor. In some areas of
Nzwani (q.v.), for example, the population (q.v.) is suffi-
ciently dense that growing tubers and legumes makes the
most efficient use of the available land.

AHMED ABDALLAH. First President of the Independent
Republic of the Comoro Islands. Born June 12, 1919, in
Domoni (q.v.) on the island of Nzwani (q.v.), he entered politics in the 1940s and served in a number of political posi-
tions prior to Comorian independence (q.v.). Prior to enter-
ing politics he had been a successful businessman and had
built a considerable fortune importing rice and sugar and exporting cloves (q.v.), vanilla (q.v.), and ylang-ylang (q.v.)
essence. The family business that he built, Abdallah et Fils,
is still an important Comorian business concern. Among the
many offices he held were Comorian Representative to the
French Assembly (1953–1959), Senator of the Comoro
Islands (1959–1972), and Territorial President (1972–1975).
Ahmed Abdallah was strongly pro-independence in the
1960s and 1970s and led the Comoros to a unilateral declaration of independence (q.v.) in July 1975. A month later, a
mercenary-assisted coup led by Ali Soilih (q.v.) removed
him from the presidency. Engaging the assistance of the
same group of mercenaries (q.v.), Ahmed Abdallah regained
the presidency in May 1978, declared the Comoros an
Islamic state, and banned political opposition. He was re-
elected in 1984. Protected by a private force of mercenaries,
he survived several coup attempts. He was assassinated in

1989 by his own mercenary force. He was a Grand Master of the Order of the Green Crescent of the Comoros and of the Order of Anjouan.

AIR COMORES. Established as a privately owned airline company at the beginning of the 1960s, by 1975 Air Comores was 51% owned by Air France and 49% owned by the Comorian state. Until the completion of Hahaia (q.v.) airport in 1975 and the weekly scheduling of jumbo jets from France to the Comoros by Air France, Air Comores was the principal airline serving the Comoros. In April 1977 Air France's shares in the airline were transferred to the Comorian state. Air Comores now operates flights to and from East Africa and Madagascar and between the islands of the Comoro archipelago. At varying times, and in response to varying political situations, service has included Dar es Salaam, Mombasa, and Majunga (q.v.).

ALAOUI I, SULTAN. Ruler of Nzwani (q.v.) from 1803, when he took over the throne from Abdallah I (q.v.), to 1823, when he died. Abdallah I had traveled to Bombay when Alaoui I claimed he was dead and took over as sultan of the island.

ALAOUI MTITI, SULTAN. Son of Sultan Abdallah II (q.v.). Also known as Alaoui II. He was the ruler of Nzwani (q.v.) between 1836 and 1840.

ALI KEMAL (PRINCE). An ambassador to France in 1980 under the Ahmed Abdallah (q.v.) government, Ali Kemal formed an opposition group, Comité national du salut public (q.v.), which demanded the resignation of Ahmed Abdallah (q.v.). He was allegedly involved in an abortive, mercenary-assisted coup attempt in 1983.

ALI SOILIH. The leader of the August 1975 coup which ousted Ahmed Abdallah (q.v.), Ali Soilih was President of the Comoros between 1976 and 1978. Born in 1936 or 1937 on Ngazidja (q.v.), he studied agronomy in France. In 1964 he became President of the Economic Development Society of the Comoros. He was elected to the Territorial Assembly in 1968 and served as Minister of Public Works from 1970 to 1972. He was a leader of the National United Front. After the August 1975 coup, he served as Minister of Defense. He then moved into a ministerial post until January 1976, when he was elected President of the Comoros by the National Council of the Revolution and the National Executive Council, succeeding Saïd Mohammad Djaffar.

Setting out on a program of sweeping changes, he attempted to completely transform Comorian culture and society, proclaiming the islands a democratic, secular, socialist republic. He outlawed expensive traditional weddings and demanded that women (q.v.) burn their *buibui* (q.v.) and *ziromani* (protective garments equivalent to veils in Islamic societies) and learn public speaking skills. He promoted the development of a Swahili-style orthography to replace Arabic script. Moreover, he created a youth corps, dismantled the civil service, redistributed land, and burned all the government records and archives. Although he banned what he referred to as "sorcery," it is alleged that he relied on the advice of his own private "sorcerer." He survived several coup attempts until May 1978, when he was overthrown by some of the same mercenaries (q.v.) who had assisted him in the 1975 coup. He was imprisoned but was killed two weeks later while "attempting to escape."

ALMADUA. One of the "clans" or royal families on Nzwani (q.v.). Based in Domoni (q.v.) and claiming descent from the Shirazi (q.v.) founders of that town, the Almadua family struggled with the Almasela (q.v.) of Mutsamudu (q.v.) for hegemony over Domoni and the entire island.

ALMASELA. One of the "clans" or royal families on Nzwani (q.v.), the Almasela were based in Mutsamudu (q.v.). Conflict between the Almasela and the Almadua (q.v.) was particularly intense during the eighteenth and nineteenth centuries; these conflicts and rivalries were occasionally exacerbated and encouraged by European trading companies. The British East India Company, for example, is said to have granted special protection to the Almasela sultans of

Mutsamudu, to have recognized the Almasela's rights over the old town and port of Domoni (q.v.), and to have helped to supress at least one slave uprising in the 1700s.

ANDRIANTSOULI. A Sakalava (q.v.) king who converted to Islam (q.v.). In 1832 he fled Madagascar and settled in Mahoré (q.v.) with his soldiers and followers. A series of conflicts ensued, both with the sultan of Mahoré and with Ramanataka (q.v.), a Merina arch-enemy of his, who had become the sultan of Mwali (q.v.). In 1835 Andriantsouli became Governor of Mahoré with the support of Sultan Abdallah of Nzwani (q.v.). Faced with continuing Betsimisaraka slave raids from Madagascar and with the continuing claim of Nzwani for domination of Mahoré, Andriantsouli ceded the island to the French in 1841 in exchange for an annual rent of 5,000 francs and the French education of his two sons. Nonetheless, he continued to maintain that he was the rightful ruler of the island. He died in 1845.

ANJOUAN see NZWANI

ARAB COUNTRIES. Relations with Arab countries were strengthened following Ahmed Abdallah's (q.v.) return to power in 1978 and the establishment of the Comoros as a Federal Islamic Republic. In particular, Arab funds helped finance a modernization program in the Comoros which included the building of roads, an international airport at Hahaia (q.v.), new power plants, a telephone system, and a deep-water port in Mutsamudu (q.v.). Arab funds also helped to expand and enlarge several mosques in the islands.

ARCHAEOLOGY. Although the digging of a new well, or the foundation for a new house or even for the expansion of an old house, can sometimes reveal a rich archaeological record in the Comoros, until recently there has been little organized archaeological investigation in the islands. Recent work has now documented traces of early Bantu African populations at Mro wa Dewa, on Mwali (q.v.); at Sima, on

Nzwani (q.v.); and at Madjikavho, on Mahoré (q.v.). These settlements, from the eighth to the tenth centuries, are typified by houses of vegetable materials (palm, wood), and by red and black bowls of what is called the "Dembeni" type. The inhabitants of these settlements also used ceramics imported from China (Yueh styles) and from the Arabian Gulf (Sassanian-Islamic styles). They made shell beads and iron implements. There is also evidence that some of these early villages included Muslim inhabitants.

AREA. The total area of the archipelago is 863 square miles (2,236 square kilometers). The area of the Federal Islamic Republic is 718 square miles (1,862 square kilometers).

ARTS. These include woodworking, embroidery, raffia weaving, and jewelry. In general, woodcarving and jewelry are men's arts, while raffia weaving and embroidery are women's (q.v.) arts. Finely carved elaborate geometric patterns cover the surfaces of doors, tables, koran holders, lamp holders, cabinets and—more recently—a large variety of tourist wares. Many buildings with little other external decoration are graced with massive carved wooden double doors. This overall geometric approach is also applied to other arts. An unusual form of embroidery requiring painstaking circular repeat-sewing is applied to white cotton *kofia* (men's hats); the result is a surface completely covered with embroidered circles, generally arranged in geometric patterns; occasionally words are hidden in the patterns. Raffia is woven into a wide variety of objects including baskets, mats, hats, tobacco pouches, and—recently—purses. The latter three items are frequently woven in multicolored geometric patterns. Also using geometric patterns as a base, fine gold and silver jewelry is worked in elaborate filigree designs reminiscent of Yemeni and South Indian styles. Recently new jewelry styles have been created using small seashells and mother-of-pearl.

ASSOCIATION DES STAGIAIRES ET ÉTUDIANTS COMORIENS (ASEC) [Association of Comorian Trainees and

Students]. Founded in 1966 by Comorian students in France. Allied in 1982 with FNUK (q.v.).

-B-

BAMBAO COMPANY see SOCIÉTÉ COLONIAL DE BAMBAO

BAMBAO SOCIETY see SOCIÉTÉ COLONIAL DE BAMBAO

BANKS. The Comoro International Bank has branches in Moroni (q.v.), on Ngazidja (q.v.); and Mutsamudu (q.v.), on Nzwani (q.v.). The French Commercial Bank of the Indian Ocean has a branch at Mamutzu in Mahoré (q.v.). No bank has a branch on Mwali (q.v.). Banks are generally open between 7:30 a.m. and 1 p.m. Mondays through Thursdays. They close early (11 a.m.) on Fridays for the Islamic sabbath.

BEJA. Thought to have been a title for petty rulers in Ngazidja (q.v.) in the past; today the word *beja* is used primarily as a derogatory term meaning an uncivilized or unruly person.

BOINA COMBO. Also known as Boina Combo ben Cheikh or Boina Combo Aboubakar, he was a nephew of Sultan Cheikh Salim (q.v.) of Nzwani (q.v.). After his uncle was assassinated in 1791, he attacked Mutsamudu (q.v.) with the aid of Malagasy mercenaries, in order to avenge his uncle's assassination and to declare himself sultan of the island. Unsuccessful in this attempt, he retired to Domoni (q.v.) where he again proclaimed himself sultan, this time of the town of Domoni. In Domoni he withstood a return attack by Sultan Abdallah I's forces.

BROTHERHOODS see TARIQA

BUIBUI. Black privacy veil typically worn by women (q.v.) on Ngazidja (q.v.). Privacy veils were outlawed during the Ali Soilih (q.v.) government.

BWANA KOMBO see BOINA COMBO

-C-

CALENDRICAL SYSTEMS. Three different calendrical systems have been used in the Comoros in recent times: The Islamic lunar calendar, the Gregorian calendar, and a traditional calendar. The lunar calendar of Islam is widely used. Its holy days, including the month of Ramadan, are celebrated throughout the islands. This calendar features a seven-day weekly cycle, with devotees setting aside each Friday morning as a special time of prayer and community, gathering together in the community's major mosque. The lunar year has 12 months; each month of 29 or 30 days begins with the approximate appearance of the new moon. Because of the difference between the lunar and solar years, the Islamic calendar retrogresses 11 days through the Gregorian calendar each year. Therefore, religious festivals and observances such as the sunrise-to-sunset fasting during the ninth month, Ramadan, begin eleven days "earlier" as compared to the Gregorian calendar each successive year. The first year in this calendrical system began on Friday, July 16, A.D. 622 of the Gregorian calendar. In 1994, Muharram 1, the first day of the Islamic calendar, fell on June 10 of the Gregorian calendar.

Political domination of the islands by France since the end of the last century has made the European Gregorian calendar an integral part of Comorian daily life. This calendar, with its 12 months of varying numbers of days, its new year beginning on January 1, ten days after the winter solstice, its holy days of Easter and Christmas, and its Sunday sabbath, have become part of the annual and weekly rhythms of life in the islands, especially for those living in the urban centers and working for the government.

A third calendrical system that has been used in the islands is based on a mathematical system and appears to be disassociated from celestial phenomena, although it may have been connected to traditional agricultural or maritime seasons in past years. It has 365 days divided into four major periods: the first three have 100 days each and the last has 65 days. Each of the 100-day periods is known as a *mongo*. The 65 days at the end of each year are considered special, and people following this calendrical system avoid participating in certain rituals (q.v.) or daily activities, such as weddings or fishing, during the period. The year is also divided into seven-day weeks. Since seven divides into 365 with a remainder of one, each new year begins one day later in the week than the previous year did. Thus, for example, if this year began on a Wednesday the next year will begin on a Thursday. The year takes its name from the day on which it began. This year would be a Wednesday year, following the example given above, and it would be followed by a Thursday year. Following this seven-year cycle means that every eighth year the year takes the name of the first one in the cycle. Using this calendrical system one calculates one's age by remembering how many years with the same name as the year one was born in have occurred, multiplying by seven, and then adding the number of years that have occurred since the year had the same name as that in which you were born. This calendrical system was more widely used in the past, and it will probably disappear altogether in the near future.

CHEIKH SALIM, SULTAN. Sultan of Nzwani (q.v.) from 1785 to 1791. An active promoter of the Indian Ocean slave trade, he was assassinated in 1791.

CHRISTIANITY. Attempts to introduce Christianity to the Comoros date from at least 1821 when the London Missionary Society sent the Reverend William Elliot (q.v.) to Nzwani (q.v.). Elliot met with little success among this predominantly Islamic population and left Nzwani in 1822. Perhaps the most successful inroads were made by French Catholics in Mahoré (q.v.). Soon after Mahoré was ceded to the French by Andriantsouli (q.v.), missionaries of the Company of Jesus established a mission and a boys' school in Dzaoudzi (q.v.), while sisters of St. Joseph established a hospital and a girls' school in the same location. In 1851 the mission and schools were transferred to the Jesuits who ran them until 1879. In 1857 the Jesuits succeeded in moving the school to Mamoutzou, across the lagoon from Dzaoudzi, where they attempted to establish a model Christian village. In 1879 control of the mission was transferred to the Holy Spirit Congregation. By 1883 the religious school was closed and replaced by a secular school. Few Muslim parents had sent their children to the mission schools. Rather, it was among the Sakalava, the creoles from Reunion, and the slaves (many of whom were from Mozambique) that the mission and its schools had the most success. Overall, Christian missionaries have had only limited impact on the predominantly Islamic population of the Comoros.

CITIES. Most Comorians live in cities, towns, or villages. There are no isolated farmsteads as in the rural United States. Over 50% of the population (q.v.) lives in cities or towns of 1,000 inhabitants or more. Another 30% live in villages of between 500 and 999 inhabitants. Fewer than 20% live in smaller population centers.

Moroni (q.v.), on the west shore of Ngazidja (q.v.), is the largest city in the archipelago. A major port and the capital since 1958, it has a population of more than 20,000 inhabitants and is a magnet for immigrants, returnees, and wage-labor migrants. The second largest city is Mutsamudu (q.v.) on the north shore of Nzwani (q.v.). Also an important port, it has a population of more than 10,000 inhabitants. Together with Mirontsi (pop. 6,000) and Wani (q.v.) (pop. 7,000), two smaller towns to the east, Mutsamudu forms one of the largest urban areas in the archipelago. The towns of Dzaoudzi, Sandangue, and Labattoir, on the islet of Pamandzi (q.v.), also form a large urban complex with a combined population of more than 10,000 inhabitants. Among the large towns, Momoju (Mamutzu), on the east coast of Mahoré (q.v.), and Domoni (q.v.), on the east shore of Nzwani, are probably the largest, with populations of 8,000 each. Iconi (q.v.), to the south of Moroni (q.v.), is the next largest, with a population of 6,000. Also with a population of 6,000, Fomboni (q.v.) is the largest town on the island of Mwali (q.v.).

There are many smaller towns, with populations of 2,000

to 3,000 inhabitants, along or near the coastal areas of the islands. Small villages, on the other hand, are usually inland, in the mountainous regions of the islands, and generally have fewer than 500 inhabitants. Nzwani is an exception to this pattern, with large towns inland as well as on the coasts. In the central zone of Nzwani, in and near the Patsi (q.v.) region, are large towns such as Bazimini, Tsembehu, Dindri, and Koni Djojo, while in the southern plateau of Nyumakele of the island are the large towns of Ada Daweni, Mremani, and Wongojuu.

CLIMATE. Although climate can vary greatly from one island to another, there are generally two major seasons: a warm and rainy season between December and April, and a cool and dry season between May and November. In addition, the combination of maritime influences and mountain terrain results in a variety of tropical microclimates. During the warm and rainy season, monsoon winds—known as *kashkazi*—bring moisture to the region from the north. Colliding with the islands' mountains, these supersaturated masses of air provide abundant rainfall (q.v.). Severe storms, and occasionally cyclones, may occur during January and February.

In the cool and dry season the prevailing winds—known as *kusi*—are from the south and southeast. Although these winds bring less moisture, there is still some atmospheric humidity, especially at the peaks of the mountains. Temperatures are affected by the surrounding sea as well as by the seasonal winds, with the sea lending a measure of stability to the climate overall.

Average temperature is 78 degrees Fahrenheit (25.3°C). Warm and rainy season temperatures average between 75 and 79 degrees Fahrenheit (24–26°C). The hottest month is March, with average temperatures of 84 to 86 degrees Fahrenheit (29–30°C). Cool and dry season temperatures average between 73 and 77 degrees Fahrenheit (23–25°C) with an average low of 66 degrees Fahrenheit (19°C). Although extremes of 100 and 32 Fahrenheit have been noted, the latter only on Mount Karthala (q.v.), in general the two seasons are differentiated more by relative rainfall than by temperature differences. In the warm and rainy season rainfall is abundant in all four islands. In the period between December and April rainfall may reach as high as 15 inches (390 mm) in a month. In the cool and dry season there is little rainfall except on some of the high, wooded plateaus. From time to time, on one or another of the islands, a brief period of rain may occur during the height of the cool and dry season (typically between July and September). Rainfall is generally heavier on the west coasts and at higher altitudes. (See also RAINFALL.)

CLOVES (*Eugenia aromatica*). Originally from the Moluccas, cloves grow wild in the Comoros and have recently become an important export crop especially on Ngazidja (q.v.) and Nzwani (q.v.), with some production also on Mwali (q.v.). Plantations (q.v.) were established by the Société Colonial de Bambao (q.v.) in the 1930s. Most of the trees are on Nzwani and Mwali; fewer are on Ngazidja, and none grow on Mahoré (q.v.) due to its drier climate. Production has expanded rapidly since 1970. In 1975 cloves accounted for as much as 30% of total exports (q.v.). By 1976 cloves were probably the largest export item from the Comoros. The government has been actively encouraging the planting of more trees. The level of production, usually high, is somewhat unpredictable. Yields tend to vary according to region, season and condition of individual trees. Although the average yield per tree is between two and five pounds, some trees may yield up to eleven pounds in particularly good years. Harvesting must be done by hand and care must be taken not to damage the branches. Ladders are used, but it is more common for pickers just to climb the trees. Prices also vary, depending on the success of crops in Zanzibar (q.v.) and Madagascar. Indonesia is the principal importer of cloves.

COCONUT (*Cocos nucifera*). Originally from Polynesia, the coconut is widely cultivated in the Comoros, particularly in the coastal regions and is probably the Comoros' principal crop. It provides food, drink, cooking oil, thatching materials, wood for building and cooking, and copra (q.v.) for export. Coconut grows easily along the coast and inland up to about

1600 feet. About 37% of cultivated land on Ngazidja (q.v.), Nzwani, and Mwali (q.v.) is planted in coconut trees. Some trees are planted in plantations (q.v.), some are individually owned. Over 77 million coconuts are produced annually. However, in some years as much as a third of the crop may be damaged by rats. Mwali is the principal island engaged in the processing of coconut flesh into copra (q.v.), and half of the drying ovens in the islands are on Mwali. In recent years Mwali was exporting over 1,500 metric tons of copra, compared to 1,000 tons in Ngazidja, 800 tons in Mahoré (q.v.) and 400 tons in Nzwani.

COELACANTH (*Latimeria chalumnae*). This unusual fish with limblike fins and a lobed tail appears to be a missing link in the evolutionary chain, intermediate between fish and land animals. It is routinely caught by Comorian fishermen in the deep waters surrounding the islands and until recently was dried and salted for food. Outside of the Comoros, however, it was known only by means of fossil remains. Western scientists therefore assumed it to be extinct. This changed, however, first in 1938 when a specimen was identified in South Africa (q.v.) and then in 1952 when a Coelacanth caught off the island of Nzwani (q.v.) was brought to the attention of western scientists. It was then recognized that they exist in the waters of the Comoro Islands. Recently, the Coelacanth has been filmed in its habitat but attempts to capture and transport a live specimen have not met with any success.

COFFEE. Small quantities of coffee are grown in the Comoros, primarily for local consumption. There is a naturally non-caffeinated variety of coffee which grows in Nzwani (q.v.) but it is quite bitter in taste.

COMITÉ NATIONAL DU SALUT PUBLIC [National Committee of Public Salvation]. An opposition movement formed in Paris in 1980 by Ali Kemal (q.v.) shortly after he declined a post in Ahmed Abdallah's (q.v.) cabinet. Ali Kemal accused Ahmed Abdallah of corruption and called for his resignation.

COPRA. The dried white meat of the coconut (q.v.), copra yields an oil used in the manufacture of soap and candles. Copra oil was a major export item from the Comoros (480 tons in 1958) until the forced closing of the oil and soap factory in 1960. Local importers, arguing that the oil produced by the Société Bambao oil mill did not meet appropriate hygienic standards, obtained a court order closing the mill. The associated soap factory was also closed. By 1963 the export of copra oil had been ended. Both soap and oil are still made locally. Individual entrepreneurs in the coastal towns— mostly women (q.v.)—make and sell copra oil, for example, but none is exported. In the meantime, copra itself has become an important export in recent years. Ngazidja (q.v.) and Mwali (q.v.) are the largest exporters of copra, each producing approximately 1,000 tons of copra per year. Mahoré (q.v.) produces 500 to 800 tons per year, while Nzwani (q.v.) only produces 400 to 500 tons per year. These figures vary significantly in response to world prices with the total export amounts varying from 1,000 to 5,000 metric tons depending on market.

CURRENCY. The monetary unit in the Comoros is the Comorian franc. The Comorian franc is directly equivalent to the Central African franc (CFA) used in many francophone African states. Like the CFA, the Comorian Franc was pegged to the French franc; until the end of 1993 fifty Comorian francs equalled one French franc. The French franc is used in Mahoré (q.v.).

-D-

DAIRA. A ceremony performed by men of the Shadhiliya sect of Sunni Islam in commemoration of a deceased relative or other important person. The Daira is performed on the seventh and fortieth nights following a death, as well as on the anniversary of the death. Daira translates roughly as "circle" and the men who participate in the ceremony stand in a circle and recite elaborate chants with shifting rhythms and multipart harmonies. Often women (q.v.) will prepare baked goods to serve at the conclusion of the ceremony.

DENARD, BOB. Born Gilbert Bougeaud in Caen, France, in 1929, Bob Denard developed an international reputation as a professional soldier. He served in the French antiguerrilla campaigns in North Africa and Indochina, fought in Zaire in 1960 and 1965, was a member of Gabon President Bongo's presidential guard, and is said to have recruited mercenaries to fight in Angola. In 1975 he allegedly assisted Ali Soilih (q.v.) in overthrowing the newly independent government of the Comoro Islands and then trained Ali Soilih's national army. In 1977 he is said to have led an abortive airborne invasion of Benin (the intent had been to topple President Mathieu Kerekou). In 1978 Denard assisted a second coup in the Comoros, overthrowing the Ali Soilih government and reinstating the Ahmed Abdallah (q.v.) government. He then established a residence in the Comoros and lived there, dividing his time between the Comoros and South Africa (q.v.), until 1989 when Ahmed Abdallah was assassinated. He moved to South Africa, and then to France.

DISEASE. Malaria is nearly endemic in the Comoros and about 80% of the adult population suffers from this disease. There is also a relatively high incidence of tuberculosis. Leprosy is still occasionally reported, although it is not as much of a problem as it was in earlier times, when the small islet to the south of Mwali (q.v.) was set aside for use as a leper colony. Children are more likely to suffer from malnutrition or intestinal parasites than from disease, but occasionally a measles epidemic breaks out among young children. In the 1980s it was estimated that one-half of all children die before reaching age four.

DJOUMBE FATIMA, QUEEN. Queen of Mwali between 1842 and 1878. Djoumbe Fatima was the daughter of Ramanataka (q.v.), the Merina ruler of Mwali. Her mother, Rovao, was also a member of the Merina royal family. When her father died, in 1842, she was five years old and her mother and stepfather ruled in her place for several years. Her stepfather, Tsivandini, had been a close advisor of Ramanataka's, and despite Ramanataka's desire for his daughter to establish relations with the French, Tsivandini pursued continued relations with Zanzibar (q.v.).

In 1847, after the divorce of Tsivandini and Rovao, the French provided a governess for Djoumbe Fatima and arranged for the 1849 coronation of the young queen. The governess was expelled in 1851 and the queen married Saïd Mohammed Nasser M'Kadar, a cousin of the sultan of Zanzibar. Although he ruled as prince consort for a decade, the French succeeded in expelling him in 1860. Djoumbe Fatima then married two Nzwani (q.v.) sultans (q.v.) in rapid succession.

In 1865 she entered into an arrangement with a Frenchman named Joseph François Lambert, assisting him in establishing a commercial presence in the island and requiring that he provide her with five percent of all profits. In 1867 she denounced the treaty with Lambert and entered into a protectorate with the sultan of Zanzibar. She then abdicated in favor of her son, Mohammed ben Saïd Mohammed. She was returned to the throne by the French in 1871, after which Lambert reestablished his commercial interests on the island. Djoumbe Fatima then ruled until her death in 1878.

DOMONI. One of the oldest of the cities in the Comoros, Domoni was the capital of the ancient sultans (q.v.) of Nzwani (q.v.). According to legend, it was founded by a group of Shirazi (q.v.) settlers. As this group explored and settled the island, they brought with them a rooster and a goat. The legend says that wherever the rooster crowed the settlers built a mosque, and wherever the goat slept the settlers founded a town. Domoni was the spot at which both the rooster crowed and the goat slept. The Shirazi mosque, on a bluff overlooking the shore, commemorates this legendary spot.

Located strategically behind a promontory on the east coast of Nzwani, with a natural harbor on each side of the promontory, Domoni grew into a major walled city and played a significant role during the Malagasy raids of the eighteenth and nineteenth centuries. Inhabitants of Domoni functioned as lookouts, sounding an alarm (usually a conch shell trumpet) as soon as war-canoes came into sight. The alarm was a signal for everyone in the area to take shelter within the walls of the city. Herdsmen would also bring their flocks into the city for protection. The capital of Nzwani was shifted to Mutsamudu (q.v.) in the late 1800s, as the result of conflicts between major branches of the ruling family.

Today Domoni has a population of more than 8,000, swelled by the recent flow of refugees from Majunga (q.v.). Momoni ("on the peninsula"), the northernmost section of the city, behind the promontory, has the oldest buildings. Hari-Ya-Muzhi ("center of town"), the appropriately named center of the city, houses the large Friday mosque and the ancient Shirazi mosque. Most of the descendants of the original Shirazi population make their homes there. While buildings in Momoni and Hari-Ya-Muzhi are primarily of the old stone and coral construction, those in Maweni ("on the rocks"), the southern section of the city, are more commonly built of thatched and tressed palm leaves. This is the area in which many of the recent immigrants built homes. A post office and market were built in the 1950s as was the home of then-senator Ahmed Abdallah (q.v.). In the 1970s several suburban western-style houses were built, as well as a hotel and a lycée. Rebuilding has also been an important part of the development of Domoni. In the early 1980s, for example, tall minarets were added to mosques including the Friday mosque in the center of town. Also, after Ahmed Abdallah's death, his house in Domoni was expanded into a memorial center.

DZIA LA NZE. A large, very deep lake on the island of Nzwani (q.v.), just below Ntingui (q.v.) peak. There are numerous local legends about this lake. It is said, for example, that the lake has no bottom. It is also said that leaves never remain on the surface of the lake.

DZIA LA UTSUNGA [Herdsman's Lake]. A small lake in the highlands of Nzwani (q.v.).

DZIANI DZAHA. A small lake on the islet of Pamandzi (q.v.), Mahoré (q.v.).

-E-

EARLIEST POPULATIONS see ARCHAEOLOGY

ECONOMY. Prior to the French colonization period, Comorians had been actively involved in the long-distance trading networks of the Indian Ocean. Sailing ships from the Comoros plied the Indian Ocean trade, and the islands also functioned as a provisioning stop for sailing ships from other nations.

In the nineteenth century French planters encouraged the development of commercial monocropping in the islands, establishing sugar and copra (q.v.) plantations (q.v.) on Mahoré (q.v.), Nzwani (q.v.), and Mwali (q.v.), and vanilla (q.v.) and clove plantations on Ngazidja (q.v.). European interest in perfume plant crops in the years following World War I encouraged colonial entrepreneurs to establish ylang-ylang (q.v.) plantations there as well. By the 1970s half of the production of essential oil in the Comoros was controlled by plantation companies such as the Société Colonial de Bambao (q.v.) or the Société Anonyme de la Grande Comore (q.v.).

Today the economy of the Comoros relies heavily on the cultivation and processing of perfume plants and spices for export. Vanilla, ylang-ylang, cloves (q.v.), and copra are the principal export crops. The Comoros are the world's leading producer of essence of ylang-ylang and the word's second leading producer of vanilla. Other, less important, export crops include coffee (q.v.), cinnamon, jasmine oil, and basilic. Potential export crops include lemon grass, black pepper, and a variety of naturally noncaffeinated coffee which has yet to be commercially developed. In earlier years sugar and sisal (q.v.) were also important crops.

The majority of the population (two-thirds) derives its principal income from fishing and agriculture (q.v.). Animal husbandry is practiced on a small scale. Individual farmers keep sheep, goats, or cattle. Fishing is also done on a relatively small scale, in spite of recent aid from Japan and cooperative agreements with European countries designed to boost fishing. The catching and sale of Coelacanth (q.v.) to museums and research centers generates some fishing-related income. In spite of the heavy reliance on agriculture, significant amounts of meat, vegetables and rice are imported.

The Comoros also import petroleum products, equipment, and construction materials. In general agriculture represents over 40% of the GDP, trade and transport activities 27%, public services 10%, and industry (q.v.) only 7%. Overall there is a negative balance of trade, with the value of imports (q.v.) at approximately twice the value of exports (q.v.). Foreign aid and assistance from private voluntary associations has helped to some extent and tourism (q.v.) is also beginning to develop as an important part of the economy. Today the principal trading partner for the Comoros is France. Until recently the Comorian franc was tied to the French franc at an exchange rate of fifty Comorian francs to one French franc. The Comoros have been an associated state of the European Economic Community since the Lomé Convention of mid-1976.

EDUCATION. Until the early years of internal autonomy, European-style education was nearly nonexistent. Koranic schools (q.v.), which had existed for centuries, were the mainstay of the Comorian educational system until the 1930s. These schools, which nearly every Comorian attends, teach the basic tenets and principles of Islam (q.v.) and basic literacy using Arabic script. Today they constitute the basis of the Comorian pre-school system. Education in the Comoros comprises two years of Koranic school, six years of primary education, three years of lower secondary education (rural college), and four years of upper secondary (lycée) education. Lycée training offers specialization in agricultural management, economics and management, teacher training, general education, housing and public works, mechanics, electricity, and health. Higher education is available only for students who are willing and able to study abroad.

In 1939 there were ten primary schools in the archipelago, and five students were selected to attend secondary school in Majunga (q.v.), Madagascar. In 1962, under the leadership of Saïd Mohamed Cheikh (q.v.) additional schools were built, bringing the total primary school capacity to 3,700 students. In the following year the first lycée in the islands was opened in Moroni (q.v.), Ngazidja (q.v.). By independence (q.v.), in July 1975, 29,000 students were attending 175 primary schools, and 4,000 students attended five junior and two senior secondary schools (colleges and lycées, respectively). By 1980 there were 56,000 students in 236 primary schools, with 12,000 more in colleges and lycées. The number of colleges had been brought up to 45, and the number of lycées to 7. In addition, the Mvuni school at Moroni, Ngazidja, now prepares teachers (especially of agriculture), as well as managers, administrators, and journalists. There is a center for artisan training in Nzwani (q.v.), and the government has plans to develop a school in Nzwani devoted the preparation of primary school teachers.

Although it remains an expensive option, students seeking higher education are still sent to other countries, usually at government expense. Most of these students enroll in higher education institutions in France and study scientific and technical subjects, but increasing numbers pursue their studies in China, Russia, Canada, The United States (q.v.), and Germany. Many of these students do not return to live in the Comoros, which results in a significant level of "brain-drain" for the islands. Between 45 and 75% of the archipelago's population now receives a basic European-style education (the figure varies from island to island), and literacy in French is estimated at 46%. One hundred percent of the population is literate in one or more of the Comorian languages (q.v.), however, due to the universal attendance at Koranic schools, where reading and writing is taught using Arabic script.

ELECTRICITY. Electrical power is supplied by Electricité et Eaux des Comores (Electricity and Water of the Comoros) and is widely available in most cities. A 220-volt current is generally provided, and European plugs are standard. A government-owned corporation, EEDC (as it is more commonly known) operates thermoelectric power stations on Ngazidja (q.v.) and on Nzwani (q.v.) where it produces 2,400 kilowatts and 1,350 kilowatts, respectively. EEDC has also recently established a 450-kilowatt generating station on Mwali (q.v.). Prior to independence (q.v.), EEDC also operated a power station on Mahoré (q.v.) with 190 kilowatts capacity. In addition, the Société Bambao has, for many years, owned and operated three hydroelectric plants in Nzwani, by which it has generated a total of 560 kilowatts for its own private use. Potential exists for hydroelectric power in Mwali but it has not yet been developed. Some hospitals, airports, and telecommunications installations have their own small generators.

ELLIOT, WILLIAM (REVEREND). An early Christian missionary to the Comoros, William Elliot was born at Sheffield, England, on September 22, 1792. A Methodist, he joined the London Missionary Society and was sent to South Africa (q.v.), arriving at the Cape of Good Hope at the end of 1820. In 1821 he was sent to Nzwani (q.v.) to establish a mission as well as to function as an official agent of Britain and to report on the activities of slave ships in the region. It is thought that he already spoke Swahili at this time. Traveling with two young Nzwani sultans (q.v.) who had been living in South Africa, Elliot arrived in Nzwani on June 20, 1821. He received little official support from the sultan of the island, had great difficulty finding a place to live and assistance in building a school, and was unable to attract many students. Attempts to proselytize among the non-Islamic population inland from the coasts were also not successful. He did manage to send reports home about slaving activities in the Comoros, and he also collected one of the earliest large wordlists of ShiNzwani, the language (q.v.) of Nzwani. Thirteen months after his arrival he left Nzwani, on the 21st of July, to return to South Africa. After a brief stay in England in 1824 he returned to the Cape in 1825 and married an African woman. They had several children together. In 1839, when Sultan Alaoui requested the installation of a British consul in Nzwani, Elliot was named to the post, but he never succeeded in finding passage to the islands. He remained in South Africa, working as a missionary, until his death in November 25, 1858.

EMIGRANTS. Emigration from the Comoros has traditionally been of a temporary nature. The traditional maritime trading culture of the the islands has always encouraged the emigration of young males, typically between the ages of 20 and 34, for the purpose of establishing trading contacts in other ports. In ancient days these young men spent much of their time at sea, sailing between the port cities of the Indian Ocean and Arabian Sea, buying and selling commodities and amassing the wealth they would need to return to the Comoros, marry and establish economic bases from which they would continue their trading activities. Although their Comorian bases were generally primary, many of these young men also established secondary bases in the ports they visited. Frequently this involved marrying in each of these ports and using these additional kin networks in their trading activities. In some cases a secondary family might have become a primary one as the amount of time spent in each location shifted.

Although individual Comorians have lived as far away as Canada and New York City, and some 15,000 Comorians were living in France in the 1960s, most have favored locations a bit closer to home. Zanzibar (q.v.) and Majunga (q.v.) were particularly popular areas for settlement, and until the anti-Comorian massacres of the 1960s and 1970s there were large Comorian communities on those islands (30,000 in Zanzibar, 35,000 in Madagascar). In fact, in the 1960s, approximately one-third of the entire Comorian population was living outside of the Comoros, and the largest Comorian city in the region is believed to have been Majunga, in northwestern Madagascar. Today with air transportation (q.v.), the old maritime trading traditions have been reinterpreted. Young men still travel on business, and many spend lengthy periods pursuing higher education in France, Russia, China, Arabia, Canada, and the United States (q.v.). Some establish families and businesses in these countries and settle down as more-or-less permanent emigrants. But most maintain close ties with the Comoros, and many continue to participate in modernized adaptations of traditional mercantile cultural patterns.

ETHNICITY. Numerous ethnic groups contribute to the diversity of the population (q.v.) in the Comoros, and there has been significant mixing among the groups. Arabs and Shirazi (q.v) are two of the major cultural groups. Particularly numerous in Nzwani (q.v.) and Ngazidja (q.v.), they had begun settling in the archipelago by the thirteenth century, establishing dynasties of ruling families in each island. Africans are predominantly of Bantu-speaking groups and include the descendants of early immigrants to the islands as well as descendants of those brought as slaves to the islands in the seventeenth through nineteenth centuries. Their cultural contributions are strong in the Comoros. Malayo-Polynesians probably arrived as early as the first Africans, if not earlier. According to legend they are the original autochthonous population of the Comoros and inhabited caves in the hillsides. Sakalava (q.v.), who arrived during the Malagasy invasions of the 1800s, have become a significant component of the population of Mahoré (q.v.). In addition there are Indian traders and European (primarily French) and Mauritian creoles. Also noteworthy are two groups of returned Comorians: the Zanzibaris, who returned, primarily to Ngazidja, during the 1960s, and the Sabenas (q.v.), who returned, primarily to Nzwani and Ngazidja, in the 1970s.

EXPORTS. The principal exports of the Comoros have always been agricultural. In the nineteenth and early twentieth centuries sugar was the predominant export from the Comoros, reaching as high as 4,000 tons in 1880. By the time the sugar mill closed in 1937, output was down to 400 tons. Copra (q.v.) oil then became a major export (480 tons in 1958), but in 1960 local importers successfully argued for the closure of the local oil mill (and associated soap factory) operated by the Société Colonial de Bambao (q.v.). Claiming that local production did not meet appropriate hygienic standards, the importers succeeded in obtaining a Comorian court order for the closing of the mill and factory. Copra oil production declined sharply after that and export ceased entirely in 1963. Both soap and oil are still made locally but none is exported. Sisal (q.v.), grown mainly in Nzwani (q.v.), was an important export until the mid-1950s, but fell off after that due to low world prices; export ceased in 1971. Mahoré (q.v.) exports some cinnamon, but there, too, low world prices have reduced the demand significantly in recent years. The principal exports today consist of essence of ylang-ylang (q.v.) and other perfume essences, copra (q.v.), vanilla (q.v.), and cloves (q.v.). Together these items account for approximately 95% of total domestic exports, with perfume essences accounting for 35% of the total. Ylang-ylang is the most important of these, making up approximately 75–90% of world demand. Making up the other 5% of domestic exports are coffee (q.v.), cocoa, cinnamon, coconuts (q.v.), wood, and wood products. Of minor significance as export items are Coelacanth (q.v.) specimens and lava gravel (used for cement production).

-F-

FAMILY. Family ties are strong in the islands, extending over several generations and producing a wide network of close kin relations. Wealthier men are expected to have multiple wives and split their time and wealth equally among spouses. In keeping with Muslim restrictions, however, a man may not marry more than four wives at the same time. Most men marry only one wife at a time but divorce and remarriage allows men to have several wives over a lifetime. Likewise, women (q.v.) who become divorced and remarry have more than one husband over their lifetimes. With multiple spouses and remarriage, families often are composed of numerous half-siblings as well as parents and children. Adoption also brings individuals into the family network; women often adopt relatives' children when they are better off than the relative or there is a marked difference in the number of children between the two families. The adopted child is treated as a regular member of the family.

There is a clearly defined division of labor within the family with females taking on the responsibilities of internal affairs of the household, including the raising of children, providing and preparing subsistence, maintaining a solid economic base for the family, and managing the house. The males have the responsibility for external affairs, including representing the group in political and religious organizations and purchasing the luxury items of the household by raising cash through their business or labor involvements outside of the household. Young children are given no responsibilities before the age of seven, when they begin Koranic school (q.v.) and begin to take on the responsibilities of adults in the household. The boys then begin a movement outside of the household and into the external world of men. While teenagers they will live with a group of boys in a bachelor quarters (usually an abandoned house or a hut built especially for them) and search for work or attend school.

Marriage and parenthood mark the entry into adulthood for the children and their entry into the responsibilities noted above for adult males and females. With the subsequent marriage of their children, individuals change their status to elder. Once an elder, the division of labor by sex tends to have less significance, and a family member's responsibilities change from working in the domestic and external economic spheres to primary involvement with religious and political concerns. Age is respected, and the elders are looked to for spiritual and worldly guidance in family matters. In return, the adults maintain the elders. This division of labor by sex and by age makes the family in the Comoro Islands a well-organized social unit. (See also MARRIAGE; MATRILOCALITY; POLYGYNY.)

FANI. A term thought to have been used in the past for petty chiefs on the island of Nzwani (q.v.). Appears to have denoted a ruler of a smaller area than a sultan might have controlled.

FISH. Fish are a major ingredient of the traditional Comorian diet along the coasts. Deep marine trenches surround the Comoro archipelago, and fish are plentiful. A wide range of small tropical fish and shellfish are caught in the shallow coastal waters surrounding the islands; the lagoon surrounding Mahoré (q.v.) is a particularly well protected location for shallow-water fishing. Just a few hundred yards from the coasts, the continental shelf drops off rapidly, providing easy access to much deeper ocean waters and much larger fish, such as tuna, mackerel, jackfish, kingfish, and shark. Fish are caught at depths up to 1,300 feet. The Coelacanth (q.v.) is also caught in these deep waters. Only caught in Comorian waters, Coelacanth specimens are now primarily sold to research centers and museums.

Traditionally, most fishing was done in dugout canoes with handlines and nets. Some canoes were manned by a single fishermen, but most were large enough to accommodate two, three, or even four individuals. Most canoes were paddled, but some were rigged with sails and, more recently, some have been propelled by small motors. It was a point of honor for a fisherman always to bring back his catch, and tales were told of fishermen being towed hundreds of miles to the east African coast by particularly large fish. Traditional fishing was primarily done at night with kerosene pressure lanterns. No one fished during full moon nights, and fishing was also avoided during the 65-day period that ended the indigenous calendrical year. (See also CALENDRICAL SYSTEMS.)

Today, with motorized boats imported from Japan, many of these traditional practices have begun to disappear. Fishing is done either night or day and at any time of the year that the weather permits. Assistance from the Food and Agriculture Organization (FAO) of the United Nations (q.v.) has helped the government to establish a small fisheries service in the Ministry of Production, Industry, Rural Development, and Environment. An increase in fishing and an expansion of inland markets for local fishermen is seen as a promising means of increasing protein consumption throughout the islands. In spite of recent aid from Japan and cooperative agreements with European nations, fishing as an industry remains on a very small scale. The annual catch has been estimated at 3,000 tons per year. The potential annual catch, with industrialization, has been estimated at 6,500 tons per year, with an additional potential of 20,000 tons of tuna within a radius of 30 miles around the archipelago. Industrialization, however, would undercut small individual fishermen significantly.

FLAG. The official flag of the Comoros is green with a white crescent moon and four stars. The moon is placed diagonally with its open side facing the upper corner opposite the hoist-side of the flag. The stars are five-pointed and form a straight line between the horns of the crescent. The configuration is symbolic of Islam (q.v.) and the four main islands of the archipelago.

FLORA. The archipelago is estimated to be host to approximately 2,000 species of flora. A recent international ethno-botanic and floristic survey team identified 38 species of *Filicineae* (ferns), 32 species of *Graminaceae* (grasses), 29 species of *Papilionaceae* (legumes), 22 species of *Euphorbiaciaes*, 18 species of *Compositae*, 15 species of *Rubiaceaes* (berries, nuts), 14 species of *Cyperaceae* (sedges), 13 species of *Mimosaceae*, 11 species of *Caesalpiniaceae* (tamarind, cassia), and 8 or 9 species of *Bignoniaceae*, *Malvaceae* (cotton, okra), *Orchidaceae*, and *Verbenaceae*. In addition, 31 monospecific families were also noted. In general, "authentic" Comorian flora (not more recent "introduced" species) appear to possess numerous affinities with those of Africa and few affinities with Malagasy, Seychellian, or Mauritian flora. The research team also collected nearly 100 species that had been previously unknown to European scientists.

FNUC see FRONT NATIONAL POUR LA UNIFICATION DES COMORES

FNUK see FRONT NATIONAL UNI DES KOMORES

FOMBONI. With a current population 5,400, Fomboni is the largest city on the island of Mwali (q.v.). It developed from a regrouping of several small towns near the northern shore which felt the mutual need for a protective rampart. The old city is divided into two sections with another section, Mlembeni, said to have been assigned to those who refused to assist in the construction of the rampart. Further south the newer sections of Mdjimbia and Masandjeni have fewer stone houses and more small huts of tressed palm leaves. To the west is Mabahoni, a section settled originally by

WaNzwani laborers for the Société Colonial de Bambao (q.v.). Today as Fomboni grows it is absorbing neighboring small towns such as Kanaleni and Bwangoma.

FONDS DE DEVELOPPEMENT ECONOMIQUE ET SOCIAL (FIDES) [Foundation for Economic and Social Development]. A French agency for the distribution of aid to the Comoros during colonial rule. In 1948 FIDES instituted a five-year plan to assist in the development of public works in the Comoros. Research and development programs were also initiated in the 1960s and early 1970s through FIDES.

FOREIGN AID. From initial colonization until independence (q.v.), France was primarily responsible for all financial aid and technical assistance to the Comoros. Following independence, in the summer of 1975, France suspended its financial aid, which at that time amounted to approximately 41% of the territorial budget. France also withdrew those services which had been financed through the metropolitan budget. By December 1975 France had withdrawn all technical assistance from the Comoros as well. This included staffing for hospitals, secondary schools, airports, and water supply systems. After a worldwide appeal the Comoros received some food and medical assistance in early 1976, but it was not sufficient and by December 1976 the United Nations (q.v.) issued an urgent appeal for economic assistance on behalf of the islands. Arab countries (q.v.) have, in general, been the primary donors of economic aid to the Comoros; some assistance has also been provided by the People's Republic of China. Recently aid has been received from European countries as well.

FORESTS. All of the islands have suffered a loss of natural forests. Most of the wood cut is used for domestic firewood, for essential oil distilleries, and for drying coconuts (q.v.) in order to produce copra (q.v.). A small percentage is also used for construction. Wood for construction is cut in the forests of Karthala (q.v.) and Nioumbadjou, on Ngazidja (q.v.); and of Ntingui (q.v.), on Nzwani (q.v.). A sawmill is operated in the southern part of Ngazidja, providing wood for local furniture and building materials factories. Little attention has been paid to replanting. Nzwani and Mahoré (q.v.) appear to be losing forests the most rapidly, causing problems in water runoff and erosion. These problems are particularly severe on Nzwani.

FRONT DÉMOCRATIQUE (FD) [Democratic Front]. An opposition group in the Comoros which, although technically banned, continued to exist during the 1980s. It was seen by some as a front for Communist activities.

FRONT NATIONAL POUR LA UNIFICATION DES CO-MORES (FNUC) [National Front for the Unification of the Comoros]. An opposition group formed in 1979 in Kenya by former members of MOLINACO (q.v.) and exiled members of Ali Soilih's (q.v.) govermnent. FNUC's principal activity was to disseminate information regarding its views of Ahmed Abdallah's (q.v.) government. It later became known as Front national uni des Komores (q.v.).

FRONT NATIONAL UNI DES KOMORES (FNUK) [United National Front of the Comoros]. Also known as FNUK—UNIKOM (Front National Uni des Komores—Union Komoro), this group was formed in 1982 by the association of the Front National pour la Unification des Comores and the Association des Stagiares et des Étudiants Comoriens (q.v.). The switch from "C" to "K" symbolized a movement away from French colonial spellings.

-G-

GAMES. A variety of card games, dominoes, soccer, and a board game with seeds (*mraha wa ntso*) are popular throughout the islands. The latter is a variant of a game that is played from Africa to Asia. The game in the Comoros consists of a wooden board about two inches thick with thirty-two depressions in four rows hollowed out on its face. Two players sit across from each other on either side of the board taking turns placing large seeds in the two rows directly in front of them. The object of the game is to capture all of one's opponent's seeds that are in his front row.

GEOGRAPHY. The Comoro Archipelago, situated at the northern end of the Mozambique Channel between Africa and
Madagascar, consists of four principal islands and numerous
islets. At approximately 12 degrees south latitude, the archipelago lies midway between Madagascar and Mozambique.
Ngazidja (q.v.), the largest of the islands, is dominated by
the active volcano, Karthala (q.v.). With an altitude of 9,186
feet (2,800 meters), Karthala's slopes are covered with
dense tropical forest interrupted by lava flows. Moroni
(q.v.), the capital, major seaport, and largest town of the islands, lies on the western shore of Ngazidja.

Nzwani (q.v.) is the second highest of the islands, the peak
of its extinct volcano reaching 5,167 feet (1,572 meters)
above sea level. The most densely populated of the islands,
Nzwani has black sandy beaches, fast-moving streams, and
dense tropical forests. Mutsamudu (q.v.), the largest town on
Nzwani and the second most important port of the archipelago, is located on a northwestern bay of the island.

To the south of Ngazidja and the west of Nzwani lies
Mwali (q.v.), the smallest of the islands. A fertile island, it
has a central mountain range which rises to 2,556 feet (790
meters) above sea level. Its chief town is Fomboni (q.v.), located on the northern shore.

Mahoré (q.v.), to the east of the other three islands, is geologically the oldest. Heavily eroded, it is the lowest of the
islands, and is characterized by slow moving streams and
mangrove swamps. It is surrounded by a coral reef.
Dzaoudzi, its chief town, is located on the islet of Pamandzi
(q.v.) off the east coast of Mahoré. Dzaoudzi was formerly
the French administrative capital of the archipelago. With a
total area of 863 square miles (552,500 acres; 2,236 square
kilometers) and an estimated 1991 population (q.v.) of more
than 476,000, the islands are among the most densely populated regions of the world.

GEOLOGY. The Comoro Archipelago is the result of volcanic
activity over the course of several periods beginning during
the last third of the tertiary era. The four principal islands, as
well as all of the neighboring islets, are exclusively consti-
tuted of volanic and coraline rocks. This makes them geologically distinct from both Madagascar and the East

African coastal region. The four islands are generally homogeneous with regard to rock formations, topography, and the processes of erosion and soil-building. Differences among the four islands are due primarily to the phase in which each arose as well as the subsequent processes of erosion on each one. Mahoré (q.v.) is the oldest, followed by Nzwani (q.v.), then Mwali (q.v.), and finally Ngazidja (q.v.). Ngazidja, as the youngest of the islands, continues to experience lava flows today. As a result of these temporal differences, each island differs with regard to permeability of the soil and the establishment of water resources. The porosity of the recent lava flows accounts for the lack of permanent rivers (q.v.) and streams in Ngazidja, for example, while Nzwani and Mahoré, much older in origin, have developed significant hydrographic networks.

GOVERNMENT. Under the current constitution, approved in an October 1978 referendum, the Comoros are a Federal Islamic Republic. There are three branches of government: executive (President and Cabinet), legislative (Federal Assembly) and judicial (Supreme Court). The President is elected universally and is the head of state. The presidential term of office is six years, with a maximum of three terms. The Cabinet is appointed by the President. The last Presidential election was held in 1990. If the office of President becomes vacant, the President of the Supreme Court serves as President of the country until an election can be held. Legislative power is vested in an elected unicameral 42-seat Federal Assembly. Laws concerning health, external trade, federal taxation, defense, education, communications, transport, federal crimes, and economics are enacted by the Federal Assembly. Members of the Federal Assembly are elected for five years. A Federal Assembly election was held in 1992. The Supreme Court is composed of three members from each island elected by island councils, two members elected by the Federal Assembly, and two members appointed by the President. Former Presidents of the Republic also serve on the Supreme Court.

Each island elects its own Governor and Island Council. Individual islands enjoy a significant measure of administrative and legislative autonomy. The constitution recognizes the autonomy of the separate islands in all matters that are not specifically designated to the federal government and mandates that government revenues be divided between the Federal government and the individual islands. The Constitution also recognizes universal suffrage for all citizens over the age of eighteen and follows a legal system based on both French and Muslim law. The constitution has been amended several times. A 1985 amendment abolished the post of Prime Minister.

GRANDE COMORE see NGAZIDJA

GREEN PARTY see UNION DEMOCRATIQUE DES COMORES

-H-

HAHAIA. Opened in January 1975, this international airport on the island of Ngazidja (q.v.) is located twelve miles north of the capital city of Moroni (q.v.). Large enough to accommodate Air France's Boeing 707s, Hahaia has made it possible to fly directly between Paris and the Comoros (generally with a stop in Djibouti or Nice).

HEALTH AND SOCIAL SERVICES. There are few health professionals in the Comoros. Most left after independence (q.v.) and have not been replaced. In 1983 there were seventeen physicians, one pharmacist, and one nutritionist in the Comoros. There is a hospital in Moroni (q.v.), one in Mutsamudu (q.v.), a small hospital in Domoni (q.v.), and a clinic on Mwali (q.v.). Life expectancy is low and infant mortality is high. Thirty-seven percent of the population (q.v.) suffers from malnutrition. Malaria is a problem, particularly on Ngazidja (q.v.). A vaccination program has been established by the government (q.v.) and the United Nations (q.v.).

HIRIMU. An age set. A group of men or women of approximately the same age who form an association for the purpose of mutual aid and companionship. The group maintains a pool of funds from which any member can borrow, assists members at important social functions such as marriages, provides assistance in the performance of tasks, and joins together to eat and dance at major rituals (q.v.).

HOTELS. Since independence (q.v.) there has been increased emphasis on the development of tourism (q.v.) in the islands. As a result the number of hotels in the Comoros has increased significantly. There are now six hotels on Ngazidja (q.v.) (double the pre-independence number), two on Nzwani (q.v.), three on Mahoré (q.v.), and one on Mwali (q.v.). In addition there are numerous pensions, guesthouses, and beach cottages for rent.

HOUSE TYPES. Houses vary from two-roomed thatched or tressed palm leaf huts to elaborate multistoried buildings of stone and coral construction. Most common are two-roomed houses attached to central courtyards. The courtyard, as the core area of a house, contains bathing and cooking areas (most cooking is still done on open hearths with wood for fuel). The interior room closest to the courtyard is generally a bedroom and serves as the semi-private quarters for the woman of the house. Another, fronting onto a public street, is reserved for entertaining. This room is often thought of as the "male" part of the house. A porch or public sitting area is a desirable addition to the street side of any house. Larger houses are generally variants of this basic pattern. Houses of more than one story generally incorporate small shops or warehouses on the ground floor and living quarters on the upper floor(s). In ancient times the ground floors of multistoried buildings were also used to house slaves and servants. Some more recently built houses incorporate modifications based on Western house-types. A few have both Western and traditional kitchens and baths.

HUMBLOT, LÉON. A French naturalist, Léon Humblot was instrumental in assisting in the colonization of the Comoros by France in the late 1800s. He was born in Nancy, France, on June 3, 1852, as Joseph-Henry Humblot, but preferred using the name Léon. As a youth he studied horticulture and obtained a job as a gardner for the Natural History Museum in Paris. Developing an interest in tropical plants, he was put in charge of a botanical research mission to Madagascar in 1878. While there he established an experimental garden and collected rare orchid species. He returned to France in 1880, donated his orchid collection to the museum, and in 1881 returned to Madagascar where he established several experimental plantations.

In 1884 the museum directed him to expand his research to the Comoros as well as to the east African coastal region. He began with the Comoros, surveying Mahoré (q.v.), Mwali (q.v.) and Ngazidja (q.v.). The political situation in Ngazidja at the time was complex. The young Sultan Saïd Ali (q.v.) was seeking domination over the island and had appealed to the French for assistance. Humblot saw Ngazidja as an ideal location to establish a plantation specializing in the production of essential oils. The two men became allies and at the age of 33, Humblot abandoned his career with the museum and settled in the Comoros as a grower and processor of perfume plants. He assisted Sultan Saïd Ali in deposing and exiling Sultan Hachim, the last ruling sultan of Ngazidja, and gradually accumulated significant amounts of power and land in the island. He organized and became the director of the colonial enterprise "Société Humblot" (Humblot Company). Eventually the company became known as the Société Anonyme de la Grande Comore (q.v.).

In 1889 Humblot convinced the French government to appoint him Résident as well. From this unique position of power Humblot gradually expanded his control over Ngazidja. By 1893 he effectively controlled 52,000 hectares, more than half of Ngazidja's land area, and in 1909 he succeded in purchasing Lambert's 5,000 hectare property in Mwali to add to his holdings. His territory included several towns, most of whose residents were indentured as slaves on his plantations (q.v.). Becoming more and more autocratic, he was eventually replaced as Résident of Ngazidja by Henri Pobeguin in 1896, but continued to direct the Société Humblot. In 1912 he was sued successfully in a

French court of law by Sultan Saïd Ali for land, money, and a complete accounting of the finances of the Société Humblot. The trial attracted worldwide notoriety for Humblot and the manner in which he had attempted to dominate Ngazidja and enslave its inhabitants. Humblot died two years later, on March 20th. He was buried in Nyumbadjuu, Ngazidja.

-I-

ICONI. Located south of Moroni (q.v.), Iconi is one of the most ancient towns of Ngazidja (q.v.). It is alleged to have been sacked by Malagasy raiders during the nineteenth century. Just to the north of Iconi is a high mountainous precipice from which the women (q.v.) of Iconi are said to have plunged to their deaths, rather than become enslaved by Malagasy slave raiders.

IMPORTS. Food and consumer goods make up the majority of the Comoros' imports. Each of these has been approximately 40% of total imports. With much of the best land devoted to export crops, the country is unable to grow sufficient food crops to provide for all its needs. In addition, the increasing number of expatriates and of Comorians returning to the islands from other countries has resulted in a strong demand for non-local foods and for luxury items. Rice, a basic dietary staple in the Comoros, is the largest single import item and at times has accounted for over 20% of total imports. Although some mountain rice is grown in Mahoré (q.v.) and Nzwani (q.v.), it is insufficient to meet local needs. Most rice is imported from Pakistan, Thailand, and Burma. Other food items are imported from Botswana, South Africa (q.v.), and Madagascar. Also imported are wheat flour, textiles and clothing, cement (although some local coral-based cement is also used), and industrial vehicles. Building materials are imported primarily from Kenya, and machinery, spare parts, and consulting services are imported primarily from France. Cars are imported from France and, more recently, have also been imported from Japan.

INDEPENDENCE. Although political movements promoting independence had existed since at least the 1960s the Comoros did not actually become independent until 1975. Prince Saïd Mohamed Djaffar (q.v.) declared independence in 1972, but this declaration was not recognized by France. A referendum was held in 1974 in which Mahoré (q.v.) voted not to become independent, while the other three islands voted overwhelmingly for independence from France. Independence was again declared, on July 6th, 1975, and this time France recognized the three islands that had voted for independence but insisted on a second referendum on Mahoré. The following year Mahoré voted overwhelmingly to remain separate from the independent Comoro Islands and to remain with France.

INDUSTRY. The distillation of essence of ylang-ylang (q.v.) is one of the principal industries in the Comoros. Other essential oils are also distilled such as basilic, lemon grass, and patchouli. Numerous spices including pepper, cloves (q.v.), cinnamon, and vanilla (q.v.) are prepared for export. A small soft-drink bottling plant in Nzwani (q.v.) relies heavily on local limes, and there is also a sawmill, a brickworks, a soap factory, and a number of small-scale, localized furniture factories which produce handmade and decorated furniture. The conversion of coconut (q.v.) into copra (q.v.) also provides some industrial employment. In the past coconut oil and sisal (q.v.) were also manufactured, but these have been abandoned.

Until fairly recently the essential oil-producing industry was controlled by just a few large groups including the Société Bambao, Etablissements Grimaldi, and Établissements Kalfane. Large-scale businesses, these groups owned the plantations (q.v.), operated the stills, and marketed the essences abroad. Frequently they were engaged in importing commodities as well. In the 1970s, however, the Comoros began to transfer land from the large estates to small farmers. Numerous small scale distilleries have been built as a result and these are operated, in competition with the larger companies, with some measure of profitability.

The wood industry provides most of the timber used for construction in the islands. Furniture and other wood products are manufactured both at small factory and at local handicraft levels, and there is a sawmill in the forest of Nioumbadjou in the south of Ngazidja (q.v.). A soft-drink bottling plant established recently in Nzwani is entirely foreign-owned. It employs 30 individuals. Although the production of soap closed down in 1960 due to pressures from importers, a new soap factory was established in 1975 in Ngazidja, bringing the manufacture of soap back to the Comoros. There is one private building company incorporated in the Comoros and it receives most of the government construction business. Most houses are built traditionally, either of wood and palm thatch, or of stone and coral cement.

INFO'COMORE. An official government information bulletin during the early 1970s. It was produced in mimeographed form, as there were no printing presses in the islands at that time.

ISLAM. The official (and predominant) religion (q.v.) of the Comoros. Comorians are Sunni Muslims following the Shafi'i school of law. Several different Tariqa (q.v.), including the Shadiliya, Qadiriya, and Rifaiya, are currently active in the islands. According to local legend Islam was first introduced to the islands in 650 A.D., not long after the Hegira of the Prophet Mohamed in 622 A.D. which marks the beginning of Islam. An individual named Mohamed Athoumani is specifically mentioned as the person who introduced Islam to the Comoros. His tomb is near Ntsaoueni on Ngazidja (q.v.).

ITSANDRA. The ancient capital of Ngazidja (q.v.), this town, just a few miles to the north of Moroni (q.v.), boasts a mosque, several royal tombs, a popular public beach, a hotel, and a stone marker which appears to have been placed as a landmark by fifteenth-century Portuguese (q.v.) mariners.

-J-

JEWS. According to legend there was an early settlement of Jews in the Comoros. This immigration is said to have occurred sometime after the legendary visit of King Solomon and his armies to the islands. Today there is no clear trace of this early settlement. However, some islanders point to specific localized dietary restrictions (not mixing chicken and milk—the taboo is even extended to coconut milk in some communities—and avoiding lobsters and other shellfish), calendrical observances (some women feel it inappropriate to sew on Saturdays, which is considered the first day of the week), and other folk customs (whenever it is necessary to sew an item of clothing while it is being worn, the wearer is admonished to chew on a piece of thread, else his or her brain might be sewn-up) as evidence for an ancient substratum of Jewish culture.

JOHANNA see NZWANI

-K-

KARTHALA. The only volcano still active in the Comoros, Karthala dominates the southern half of Ngazidja (q.v.). Its most recent eruption was in 1977, when lava flows destroyed two villages and one town, displacing approximately 500 families.

KAWENI RIVER. A river in Mahoré (q.v.), the Kaweni meanders in a southeasterly direction, passing the town of Kaweni and exiting to the sea to the north of Mamutzu.

KORANIC SCHOOL. Widespread in the Comoros, Koranic schools are primarily devoted to teaching the basics of Islam (q.v.) to the population. Nearly every young child in the Comoros attends a Koranic school in his or her neighborhood and learns to read and write. For centuries Comorians have applied the Arabic script learned in Koranic schools to the writing of their own language(s) (q.v.). As a result there is a long-standing tradition of universal literacy in the Comoros. As French schools began to be introduced into the Comoros, beginning in the 1930s, Koranic schools began to function as pre-schools for increasing numbers of the population. Today between 45 and 75% of Comorians attend French schools as well as Koranic schools, becoming literate in French as well as in Comorian.

KWALE RIVER. This river in Mahoré (q.v.) meanders from above the town of Kwale in a generally easterly direction before exiting to the sea.

-L-

LAND OWNERSHIP. Prior to colonization most lands were held by the sultans (q.v.) of the islands and were divided into large private landholdings, plantations (q.v.), and village reserves. Village reserves were land that had been set aside by the sultans for their dependents so that they could establish gardens and pasture their animals. They eventually developed into commonly held lands, which inhabitants of certain villages could use for planting and pasturing according to their needs. Most such lands were assigned to families rather than to individuals.

Two colonial decrees on land ownership changed all of this dramatically. These decrees, on February 4, 1911, and September 28, 1926, established that the rights of individuals to land could be guaranteed by the process of registration. Registration was to authorize, provisionally at first, and definitively, after 30 years, the ownership of the lands granted. All lands not appropriated in this way were to be placed into government reserves, from which they could be assigned to individuals or to colonial commercial societies. Written and disseminated in French, these new laws clearly favored those who were able to read French and to complete the registration procedures. The French colonists and the colonial commercial societies proceeded to register the very largest land parcels for themselves. The colonial government then reserved the rest for itself, replacing the ancient sultans and feudal lords.

Although sultans and feudal lords had given local inhabitants rights to land-use by means of verbal contracts, the colonial government and the commercial societies were unaware of these contracts and generally did not care about them anyway. This led to situations in which farmers claimed ownership of trees that they had planted on lands which did not (under the new rules) appear to belong to them. The traditional Comorian system had allowed for such situations, but the European colonists had different conceptions of private ownership of land. Eventually small parcels were set aside for village reserves as in the old system, but the parcels were much smaller than in the traditional system. Although the amount of land owned by the colonists decreased over the years, a survey in 1966 revealed that individual colonists still owned 4.8% of the land in the Comoros, and the colonial societies owned an additional 12.8% of the land. Common village reserves and individual Comorian land ownership accounted for only 42.8% of the total land, while 39% belonged to the state. Generally, most of the best agricultural lands were still owned by colonial interests.

Today the immense plantations are in the process of disappearing. Some non-cultivable lands are being settled by squatters, and lands which can support cash cropping are being acquired by comorian entrepreneurs. In some cases the colonial societies sold the land outright to individuals; in others local administrations took over the land and apportioned it to individual farmers in ways that appear somewhat closer to traditional practice.

LAND USE. Approximately 10% of the land in the Comoros is used for growing food crops. This figure is highest (14%) on Mwali (q.v.) and lowest (8%) on Mahoré (q.v.). In contrast, 33% of the total land is used for cash crops: 45% on Ngazidja (q.v.) and 10% on Nzwani (q.v.). Only a small amount is reserved for pasturing animals (2.5% overall, 5% on Nzwani and Mahoré and almost none on Mwali). The remaining land is occupied by forests (q.v.) (43%) and other features such as rivers (q.v.), mangrove swamps, and roads (12%). Nzwani is the most heavily forested (70%), while Ngazidja is the least wooded (26%). Although it is theoretically possible to double the amount of land given over to food cropping, one would have to take special measures to prevent erosion of newly cleared land, due to the steep sloping nature of most of the land.

LANGUAGE(S). French and Arabic are the official languages of the Comoros. In addition there are four distinct indigenous varieties of Comorian spoken in the islands (ShiMahoré, ShiMwali, ShiNgazidja, ShiNzwani). Each refers, in its name, to the island in which it is spoken. ShiMahoré is the language of Mahoré (q.v.), ShiMwali is the language of Mwali (q.v.), ShiNgazidja is the language of Ngazidja (q.v.), and ShiNzwani is the language of Nzwani (q.v.). Although there are similarities among the four languages, no one language is common to all four islands. Rather, all four can be said to belong to a generalized Comorian language group and the abstract concept of a common language is expressed by the indigenous word *shimasiwa* (the word for island is *siwa*—the plural is *masiwa*—in all four languages). All four languages share a common Bantu grammatical substrate. Each has specific syntactic variants which serves to differentiate it from the others. In addition, there is a significant amount of lexical borrowing from contact languages such as Swahili, Arabic, French, English, Portuguese (q.v.), and Malagasy. Some consider ShiMahoré and ShiNzwani similar enough to be dialects of a single language, but ShiMahoré is distinguished by the presence of a large number of Malagasy loan-words. Recent concern with political unity has resulted in an emphasis on linguistic commonalities rather than differences. A common orthography has been developed which attempts to take into account all of the phonemic variation between the languages. Significant grammatical differences between the languages continue to form a barrier to unifying the languages into one. Moreover, it seems likely that the status of Mahoré as a separate political entity may eventually result in linguistic separation from the other three islands.

LEGENDS. Historical legends in the Comoros generally refer to visiting dignitaries and very early immigrations. They include stories about the throne of the Queen of Sheba and an ancient Jewish immigration to the islands. The throne of the Queen of Sheba, for example (in some versions it is her ring instead), is alleged to have been stolen by djinns and hidden in the crater of Karthala (q.v.). This is said to have resulted in a visit to the Comoros by King Solomon who, along with his armies, succeeded in retrieving the throne (or ring) and returning it to the Queen. The immigration of the Jews (q.v.) is suppposed to have followed this visit; some highly localized practices such as not mixing chicken and milk in the same dish, not sewing on Saturdays, and not eating shellfish are pointed out by some as remnants of the culture of these early immigrants. Other legends, referring to somewhat more recent times, include stories of the Shirazi (q.v.) immigration and of the settling, building, and naming of various towns and mosques.

-M-

MAHINDRINI. An extinct volcanic cone to the northwest of the town of Domoni (q.v.) on the island of Nzwani (q.v.), this is an exceptionally fertile area. Traditionally it was used as a public access planting area by area inhabitants.

MAHORÉ. Referred to by the French as Mayotte, Mahoré (or Maore) is geologically the oldest of the islands and appears the most eroded. The island, along with several satellite islets, is surrounded by a coral reef which is about a mile wide. Only two passages permit the entrance of large ships, thus providing a secure harbor. With an overall size of 144 square miles (37,000 hectares; 91,000 acres), it has a population of more than 35,000 inhabitants. Largely agricultural, the island produces more than 3,000 hectares (8,000 acres) of sugar cane. Vanilla (q.v.), ylang-ylang (q.v.), cloves (q.v.), copra (q.v.), and cinnamon are also produced. In recent years Mahoré has produced the majority of the archipelago's cinnamon. A particular variety of fragrant dry rice is also grown on Mahoré, and cattle production is an important part of the economy.

Mahoré's towns are quite different from those of the other islands. There are no walled cities, no narrow, winding streets. Instead towns are primarily comprised of wattle-and-daub or tressed coconut-frond huts ranged along wide, open streets.

The Portuguese (q.v.) were the first Europeans to see Mahoré, having sailed to the island in the early years of the sixteenth century. Soon after, in 1595, an Englishman landed on the island, but it was the French who became the dominant European influence. Of the four islands, Mahoré was the first to become a protectorate of France. In 1841 the Sakalava (q.v.) king Andriantsouli (q.v.), who had declared himself sultan of Mahoré, ceded it to the French in exchange for an annual rent of 5,000 francs and the French education of his two sons. At that time Mahoré, with a population of roughly 3,000 inhabitants, was constantly under siege by slave merchants from Madagascar. In addition, the sultan of Nzwani (q.v.) maintained that he was the rightful ruler of Mahoré as well as of Nzwani. At Adriantsouli's death, one of his sons was named ruler by the remaining Sakalava chiefs in Mahoré, but the French refused to recognize him.

In 1847, after withstanding a series of revolts, the French divided Mahoré into "concessions," and the majority of the land was taken from the Sakalava and the indigenous ruling classes and awarded to French and creole planters from Réunion. Plantations (q.v.) were established, sugar was planted, and slaves were imported, primarily from Mozambique. Much of the administration of the island was carried out from the relative "safety" of Dzaoudzi, on Pamandzi (q.v.) islet. Mahoré was grouped with the other three Comoro Islands as a French colony in 1912. In the 1940s when the Comoros were recategorized as an overseas territory of France, an official administrative center for the territory was established in Dzaoudzi. In 1962 the administrative offices were moved to Ngazidja (q.v.).

In the 1974 referendum, Mahoré voted to remain with France, rather than to become independent along with the other three islands. A second referendum was held in 1976, after the independence of the other three islands had been internationally recognized, in which Mahoré reaffirmed its intent to remain with France rather than to join with an independent Comoro Islands. Mahoré was retained by France as a "collectivité territoriale." Although it is an overseas dependency of France Mahoré still campaigns for the granting of "département" status, which would mean full citizenship status. France did not invest much in Mahoré for several years after Comorian independence, primarily in order not to alienate the Comoro government. However, after 1968, when Jacques Chirac was appointed prime minister of France, France began a major development program in Mahoré. This program included new housing, a deep-water harbor, an extended airport, jobs, land reform, and new labor laws.

MAJUNGA. In the 1960s this city on the northwest coast of Madagascar was the largest Comorian city in the Indian Ocean. The scene of a thriving mercantile community, it housed generations of Comorian traders and shopkeepers. Partly as a result of the administrative attachment of the Comoros to Madagascar and partly because of its proximity to the Comoros, large numbers of Comorians had emigrated to Majunga during the twentieth century forming a large Comorian-Malagasy population. Generations of children born in Majunga had never been to the Comoros. Some no longer spoke any Comorian languages (q.v.). Yet, like many immigrant groups the world over (but especially those whose members are traders and shopkeepers), the Comorian community in Majunga was always regarded as intrusive by local Malagasy residents of the area. The community was largely decimated in 1977 as the result of an anti-Comorian riot, and most of the survivors were transported to the Comoros.

MALAGASY REPUBLIC. Relations with Madagascar have always been stormy. Beginning in 1793 and lasting at least until 1820, war-canoes from the north of Madagascar raided the Comoros in search of slaves. Towns such as Dzaoudzi, on Mahoré; Domoni (q.v.) and Mutsamudu (q.v.), on

Nzwani (q.v.); Fomboni (q.v.) on Mwali (q.v.); and Iconi (q.v.), Moroni (q.v.), Itsandra (q.v.), Ntsoudjini, Ntsaoueni, Mitsamiouli, and Bangoi-Kouni on Ngazidja (q.v.) were heavily fortified during these years, but the population was devastated and significantly diminished. Residents of Iconi on Ngazidja still tell of the women (q.v.) who leaped off of a high promontory and into the sea, preferring suicide to slavery. Towards the end of the period of slave raids, a number of Malagasy princes settled in the Comoros and, sometimes in bloody wars, seized power in a number of locations. In several cases, it was these Malagasy rulers who turned the individual Comoro Islands over to French colonial rule. From 1912 until 1946 the Comoros were attached to Madagascar and administered from that island. Local administrators were provided little support, health and education were neglected, and the powerful colonial commercial societies effectively became the "rulers" in the islands, intervening in such issues as the selection and recall of local administrators and bureaucrats. Comorians were used by France to quell a revolt in Madagascar in 1948, resulting in a persisting unease between residents of the two nations. Most recently a large settlement of Comorians in Majunga (q.v.), in the northwest of Madagascar, was the scene of a particularly bloody massacre. Surviving Comorians fled in large numbers to the Comoros, adding significantly to the population (q.v.) pressure already experienced in these small islands. (See also ANDRIANTSOULI; RAMANATAKA; SABENAS.)

MANYAHULI. Land held communally by the children of a woman; rights to the land are transmitted through the daughters.

MAORE see MAHORE

MARRIAGE. Marriage generally begins the transition of young people into full-fledged adulthood in Comorian society. The process of transition is not normally considered complete until the couple have produced a child. Many first marriages are arranged by the parents of the couple, in consultation with a fundi (expert on astrology). Cousin marriage is preferred. Although the individuals involved are generally consulted, some adolescents come to regret agreements that they committed themselves to as children.

Marriage ceremonies are elaborate in the Comoros, particularly if they represent the first (arranged) marriage of a young man, but occasionally, as on Ngazidja (q.v.), a man's second or third marriage may be his most elaborate marriage. In this case it is the time it takes to amass the necessary wealth to host a "Grand Marriage" that determines the timing of the ceremony. In either case, these elaborate marriage ceremonies are occasions on which large numbers of people are fed and entertained in a complex web of social obligations and reciprocities. The Grand Marriage in Ngazidja generally lasts nine days and includes a *djaliko* (parade of men), a *twarab* (concert), and a *zifafa* (procession in which the husband is installed in his wife's house and in which large amounts of gold jewelry are presented by the husband to the wife). Elaborate marriages on Nzwani (q.v.), although not referred to as "Grand," generally last for three weeks and include feasts, dances, processions, prayers, ritual baths, and presentations of jewelry, furniture, household goods, and staple foods such as rice and flour in sufficient quantity to last for a year. The ceremonies in Domoni (q.v.) traditionally included a bull-run for young men. In a traditional Comorian wedding men and women celebrate separately from one another. Although such marriages are expensive, they are an important part of the system of redistribution and reciprocity. An attempt to outlaw expensive weddings by the Ali Soilih (q.v.) government in 1976–78 was resisted and resented by the general public, and the ceremonies were reinstated after the 1978 coup. (See also FAMILY; MATRILOCALITY; POLYGYNY.)

MATRILOCALITY. A pattern of residence at marriage (q.v.) in which the married couple lives with the wife's family. It was traditionally combined with polygyny (q.v.) in the Comoro Islands creating a relatively rare form of marriage in which a man with more than one wife would spend equal time visiting each wife's household. Thought to be associated with conditions in which men spend lengthy periods of time away from the community, it was ideally suited to the traditional long-distance maritime trade characteristic of the western Indian Ocean for centuries. By the time a young woman is ready to marry, her parents will have built a house, or an extension of their own house, for her to live in with her spouse. The house (or portion) becomes her property and, together with her landholdings, provides her with much of her economic base. A woman expects her husband to be engaged in long-distance maritime trade or a modern equivalent thereof, and she may provide him with an initial investment from this base in order to help him establish himself in the world market. In turn, he is expected to make occasional visits to the household, bringing the profits of his ventures home and adding to the overall economic base of the couple. As Islamic law permits a man to marry as many as four wives, those men who do so are expected to divide their time and profits as equitably as possible among the households into which they have married. (See also FAMILY.)

MAYOTTE see MAHORÉ

MERCENARIES. A strong presence in the Comoros between 1975 and 1989, mercenaries participated in coups and coup attempts, served in personal police forces, and established an international mercenary training camp in the islands. The first coup in which they participated was that of 1975. Commissioned by Ali Soilih (q.v.), mercenaries deposed Ahmed Abdallah (q.v.) as president just one month after the Comoros had unilaterally declared their independence (q.v.) from France. Three years later, commissioned by Ahmed Abdallah, they deposed Ali Soilih and returned Ahmed Abdallah to the presidency. Following this second coup a number of mercenaries "retired" in the Comoros. Many took Comorian wives, began families, and served in Ahmed Abdallah's private guard. An international training camp for mercenaries was established at the old Foreign Legion post north of Itsandra (q.v.). The mercenary presence resulted in the expulsion of the Comoros from the 1978 conference of the Organization of African Unity (q.v.). When some of Ahmed Abdallah's mercenaries were implicated in his assassination, international pressure forced the mercenaries to leave the Comoros.

MOHÉLI see MWALI

MOLINACO see MOUVEMENT POUR LA LIBÉRATION NATIONAL DES COMORES

MORONI. The capital of Ngazidja (q.v.), as well as of the Federal Islamic Republic of the Comoros, Moroni has an ancient shallow-water port; a large and ancient mosque; the central post office for the Comoros; numerous administrative buildings, including the tribunal and the Chamber of Deputies; a lycée; a hospital; an airport; several hotels (q.v.), restaurants, and clubs; a large open-air market, and a large and densely packed shopping area. According to oral tradition, it was founded during the time of the warring sultans (q.v.), when one of the sultans moved his camp a few miles to the south of the coastal area of Itsandra (q.v.). Awakened one morning by the crowing of a rooster he decided to establish a town on the site and built a mosque there of lava stones and coral.

By 1876 the town of Moroni was the capital of Sultan Saïd Ali (q.v.). At that time the town had grown to seven hectares in size and included two residential quarters, Mtsangani and Badjanani. In addition there were two protective buffer-zones primarily inhabited by servants and slaves, Irungudjani to the south and Djumwamdji to the west and north. At the end of the nineteenth century the Société Humblot installed its commercial agency at the north and south peripheries of the old town, while the European colonists created suburban residences along the roads in Dashe to the east and Magudju to the north. A market was built in 1925, a hotel (Karthala) in 1944, and a hospital and lycée in 1956. By 1958 Moroni had a population of 6,500 inhabitants.

When the territorial capital was transferred to Moroni from Dzaoudzi in 1963, the town began to grow rapidly. Suburbs such as Basha, Itzambuni and Zilimadju developed to the south near the airport, hotel, and lycée, while government officials, bureacrats, and the newly emerging professional classes developed the trendier suburbs of Hadjudja,

Ambassadeur, and Coulée de Lave (Lava-Flow) to the north, near the administrative and government buildings, the hospital, and the pharmacy. In addition to the new public buildings, houses and businesses were built in the new areas, and additional floors were added to the houses in the central part of the city. Today Moroni covers more than 200 hectares and has a population of more than 20,000. As the seat of both the federal and provincial governments, it serves important administrative and political functions. In addition, the presence of the lycée Saïd Mohamed Cheikh and the école d'enseignement supérior of Mvuni create a lively intellectual scene. Moroni is particularly important as a commercial center as well, as more than 60% of the island's exports (q.v.) pass through Moroni. The capital attracts many immigrants from the other islands as well as from the rural areas who come to work as laborers, entrepreneurs, public servants, and household employees. In addition, more than 1,000 foreigners live in the city, drawn there by international political and commercial interests.

MORTALITY RATE. The infant mortality rate dropped from an estimated high of 144.0 per 1,000 in 1969 to an estimated 95.0 per 1,000 in recent years. The estimated average annual death rate dropped from 17.2 per 1,000 in 1975–1980 to an 14.5 per 1,000 in 1985–1990.

MOUDRIYAS. These were intended to be community level administrative units in the governmental hierarchy proposed by Ali Soilih (q.v.) in the 1970s. Ali Soilih envisaged developing this hierarchy to replace the French colonial system of prefectures and cantons. Each moudriya was to have had about 6,000 people as members and was to have progressively taken over most of the decision-making and responsibility for marketing of crops, agricultural extension work, primary and lower secondary education, health, and a variety of other local services. Each moudriya was to have a local building as its administrative center, and in 1976 an intensive building program was begun in order to provide moudriya centers and offices. This boosted the construction industry dramatically, but put a great financial burden on central government. By May 1978, when Ali Soilih's government was overthrown, 57 moudriya offices had been built.

MOUVEMENT POUR LA LIBÉRATION NATIONAL DES COMORES (MOLINACO) [Comorian National Liberation Movement]. The first activist group in the movement towards independence (q.v.), MOLINACO was formed in 1962. Founded in Dar es Salaam among Comorian expatriates, it sought the withdrawal of the French and immediate independence for the Comoros. It was recognized and assisted by the Organization of African Unity (q.v.), but had difficulty establishing a firm base of support in the islands. In 1972 MOLINACO supported the establishment of the Parti pour l'Évolution des Comores (PEC) (q.v.) in Moroni.

MOUVEMENT POUR LA RÉNOVATION ET L'ACTION DÉMOCRATIQUE (MOURAD) [Movement for Renovation and for Democratic Action]. A political party founded in 1990 after the multiparty system was reinstated by Saïd Mohamed Djohar (q.v.).

MRO WA MUTSAMUDU [Mutsamudu River]. One of the larger rivers of Nzwani (q.v.), Mro wa Mutsamudu runs in a northerly direction, from the center of the island, and passes through the town of Mutsamudu (q.v.) as it exits to the sea.

MUSIC. A unique combination of bardic traditions from the Middle East, Bantu traditions from East Africa, and Malayo-Polynesian traditions from Madagascar, the traditional music of the Comoro Islands is distinctive and varied. Men's music is characterized by solo singers, or occasionally by two or more singers together, accompanied by instruments such as the five-stringed gabus, four-stringed violin, or ten-stringed box zither. Women's music is characterized by group participation, although solo commentary in song is also heard; it is generally accompanied by gongs and single frame drums or tamborines. Some spirit possession music is performed with a box zither and raft rattle, some with drums, and some (e.g., the daira) with *a capella* group chanting. Stylistic forms include through-composed solo structures, group call-and-response songs, and stanzaic compositions of three, four, or more lines per verse. One traditional form is nearly identical with classic twelve-bar American blues.

MUTSAMUDU. The capital of Nzwani (q.v.) and the site of the British Consulate in the 1800s. The current population of Mutsamudu is approximately 13,000. According to legend a herder named Musa Mudu (Black Moses) pastured his herds at the base of the bay of Nzwani, on the slopes of Hombo. There, where the grass was plentiful and the river flowed continually, Musa Mudu built his dwelling. In time, as others settled in the same region, a town grew which was eventually named for its first settler. In the eighteenth century, with the help of the British, Sultan Abdallah I (q.v.) built the Citadel overlooking Mutsamudu in order to protect the city from Malagasy invasions. Over time cannons were provided by both the British and the French. During the slave rebellion of 1891 the Citadel was taken over temporarily by slaves. The ancient town of Mutsamudu was comprised of three central sections (Hamumbu, Mdjihari, and Hampanga) surrounded by a protective rampart, and three outlying areas (Habomo, Bandamadji, and Gungwamwe) inhabited by servants and slaves. Within the rampart were the houses of the nobles and their families, the Grand Mosque, the sultan's palace, and the public square (all in Hamumbu), the fishermen's quarters (in Mdjihari, or center-of-town), and the free laborers, craftsmen, and merchants (in Hampanga, or town-square).

MWALI. Referred to by the French as Mohéli, with an area of 81 square miles (211 square kilometers), Mwali is the smallest of the islands in the Comoro archipelago. The island has rich soil, magnificent forests (q.v.) and fine pasture lands. The valleys and slopes of the island are covered with coconut (q.v.) trees, coffee (q.v.) trees, cacao and ylang-ylang (q.v.) trees, and a wide variety of crops. Three small islets on the south side of the island near the harbor of Nioumachoua provide a natural sheltering place for sailing ships during inclement weather. In the past one of these islands—Chissioua Ouenefou—was used as a leper colony. With a population of approximately 30,000, Mwali is the least densely populated (370 inhabitants per square mile) of the four islands.

The history of Mwali is complex. Controlled by Nzwani (q.v.) until the nineteenth century, Mwali was ravaged by bloody wars until 1828, when it fell into the hands of the Merina general, Ramanataka (q.v.). A brother-in-law of the Malagasy king Radama I, Ramanataka had fled from the po-litical intrigues of Madagascar and settled in Nzwani with the aid of Sultan Abdallah II (q.v.). As sultan of Mwali, he converted to Islam (q.v.) and changed his name to Abderrahman. Although he flew the flag of Zanzibar (q.v.) for a while, he advised his young daughter to depend on the French for advice and protection. When he died in 1842 his daughter, Djoumbe Fatima (q.v.), also known as Sudi, was only five years old. Her mother Rovao, also of Merina roy-alty, ruled in her place for a while, but soon found herself sharing the power with a close advisor of Ramanataka's named Tsivandini. Also of Malagasy descent, Tsivandini married Rovao in 1843, became Djoumbe Fatima's tutor, and consolidated his own power over the island. He also began making arrangements for Djoumbe Fatima's eventual marriage to a sultan of Zanzibar, in order to formalize rela-tions with that island.

The French, who had just acquired Mahoré (q.v.), were interested in developing a presence in Mwali as well. In 1847, a year after Tsivandini and Rovao were divorced, the French arranged for Madame Droit, a former friend of Rovao's, to serve as a governess for the young queen. Tsivandini and his new wife renewed their attempts to find a Zanzibari husband for Djoumbe Fatima. In 1849 the French arranged for the coronation of the young queen, re-minded her of her father's advice to rely on them for advice and support, and proclaimed that she was free to choose her own spouse. Tsivandini then left for Zanzibar.

In 1851 Madame Droit was expelled from the island. Soon after, Saïd Mohammed Nasser M'Kadar, a cousin of the sultan of Zanzibar, arrived in Mwali as a suitor, and Djoumbe Fatima agreed to marry him. As prince consort,

Saïd Mohammed Nasser M'Kadar took over much of the power and controlled most of the commercial activity in the island. In 1860 the French succeeded in expelling the prince. Djoumbe Fatima then married two Nzwani sultans in rapid succession and finally, in 1865, entered into an arrangement with a Frenchman named Joseph Lambert, assisting him in establishing a commercial presence in the island and requiring that he provide her with 5% of all profits. In 1867, however, the queen denounced all treaties with Lambert, entered into a protectorate with the sultan of Zanzibar, and abdicated in favor of her son, Mohammed ben Saïd Mohammed.

The French reestablished their presence in 1871, Lambert returned to Mwali, and Djoumbe Fatima was returned to the throne. Two years later, when Lambert died, the British-based Sunley (q.v.) interests in Nzwani took over his concessions. The Germans, too, began to show an interest in Mwali at about this time. Djoumbe Fatima ruled until her death in 1878; the second of her sons, Abderrahman, took over the sultanate. He ruled until 1885. In 1886 the French imposed a formal protectorate over Mwali. Salima Machamba was installed as queen and the French resident attempted to rule through her. The daughter of Djoumbe Fatima and her fourth husband, French sea captain Emile Feuriot de Langle, Salima Machamba had been raised in a convent in Réunion. In 1901 she ceded Mwali to France, married a French gendarme, and left with him to live on a farm in southern France. Mwali was formally annexed by France in 1912.

-N-

NDZUANI see NZWANI

NEWSPAPERS. The leading newspaper in the Comoro Islands is the weekly *Al-Watwan*. Containing items in both French and ShiNgazidja, it is published in Moroni (q.v.), Ngazidja (q.v.). Other Comorian publications include *Archipel, Miandi, Mwangaza, Perspectives Comoriennes, Le "Comorien,"* and *Le Journal de Mayotte*.

NGAZIDJA. Referred to by the French as Grande Comore, Ngazidja is the largest of the islands in the Comoro archipelago with an area of 442 square miles (1,146 square kilometers). The northern two-thirds of the island are dominated by a rocky plain known as La Grille. The southern third of the island is dominated by an active volcano, Karthala (q.v.), which is 9,186 feet (2,800 meters) in height. Karthala's crater is nearly a mile in diameter, making it the largest active crater in the world. Since 1857 there have been over a dozen eruptions with lava flows; the most extensive was that of 1918. The most recent serious eruption was in 1977. The island's population is predominantly Arab and African. Agriculture (q.v.) on the island is generally limited to areas lower than 2,000 feet in altitude. Above this altitude is a dense tropical forest (in the south) and an area of grassy plain (in the center and north).

European sailing ships stopped for provisions at Ngazidja as early as 1570. The island was ruled by 12 sultans (q.v.). Although each was independent of the others, they generally recognized a principal sultan, whose rights and responsibilities were primarily conciliatory in inter-regional disputes, and accorded him or her the title of Sultan Thibé. There was frequent conflict over the right to use this title, especially after the Europeans appeared on the scene, as these latter generally assumed that the title indicated sovereignty over the entire island.

The best documented of these conflicts is the long and complicated struggle between the sultans of Bambao and Itsandra (q.v.) during the nineteenth century. Partly in response to the Malagasy raids of the early 1800s, the sultan of Bambao appealed for aid to the Portuguese (q.v.), to the British, to Nzwani (q.v.), and to Mahoré (q.v.). The sultan of Itsandra, in turn, appealed for aid to the Merina, specifically Ramanataka (q.v.) and his soldiers, in Mwali (q.v.). In 1843 the French commander of Mahoré visited Ngazidja and established connections with Saïd Achmet, the sultan of Bambao. When Saïd Achmet died in 1875 the French then recognized Saïd Ali (q.v.) as sultan of Bambao, and as Sultan Thibé as well. Saïd Ali had received a French education in Mahoré and was opposed by the other sultans of the island, who by then had begun to prefer connections with Zanzibar (q.v.) to connections with France. Nonetheless by 1883 Saïd Ali had fought his way to establishing sovereignty over the island and granted a commercial concession to Léon Humblot (q.v.), a French naturalist. Humblot extracted an agreement from Saïd Ali that gave him ownership of any land he wished to cultivate. In return he promised 10% of the profits to Saïd Ali. Eventually Humblot owned more than half of the island.

The agreement was not popular in Ngazidja and resulted in an appeal from the sultan of Badjini, south of Moroni (q.v.), to the Zanzibaris and the Germans for assistance. When the Germans arrived with a flag and flew it at the citadel of Foumbouni, the French responded by shelling Foumbouni. The Germans withdrew. France then established a protectorate over Ngazidja and installed a Résident there. Local resistance to Saïd Ali and the French continued, and by 1893 Saïd Ali fled to Réunion, although he did not abdicate his position as Sultan Thibé.

In 1892 the French appointed Humblot Résident of Ngazidja and from then until 1896 he succeeded in acting in the capacity of principal ruler of the island. By 1896 complaints about Humblot's despotism moved the French to replace him as Résident and to attempt to force him to return land to the inhabitants of Ngazidja. Humblot resisted until 1912, when he lost a suit filed by Saïd Ali in France for his portion of the proceeds Humblot had promised in the original agreement. Saïd Ali then ceded Ngazidja to France and abdicated as Sultan Thibé. In 1914 France finalized the merger of Ngazidja with Madagascar. The company Humblot had founded, however, continued to exert significant influence over affairs of the island until after World War II.

NIOUMAKELE. The southern region of Nzwani (q.v.), it was controlled by a planter named Moquet who enslaved the villagers for work on plantations (q.v.) there. A revolt in 1940 led to eventual governmental reforms such as the 1946 proposed nationalization of non-cultivated lands.

NTINGUI. The central peak of Nzwani (q.v.), 5,167 feet (1,575 meters) in altitude, Ntingui is covered in dense vegetation.

NZWANI. Referred to by the French as Anjouan and by early English visitors as Johanna, Nzwani has also been called the "pearl" of the Indian Ocean. A triangle of approximately 50 miles on each side, it has a total area of 164 square miles (424 square kilometers). With a population of 210,000, it is the most densely populated island in the archipelago (over 1,280 persons per square mile). Its volcanic peak, Mount Ntingui (q.v.), 1,575 meters high, is covered with vegetation, in contrast with the three points of the triangle, which are less luxuriant. Nzwani is the premiere producer of essential oils inlcuding ylang-ylang (q.v.), jasmine, cassis, basilic, palmarosa, and orange flower.

Ruled by petty chiefs known as Fani (q.v.), an Arabic-style sultanate developed in Nzwani as early as the sixteenth century. Two separate groups were involved in this development. The Almadua (q.v.) were the earliest, arriving in the sixteenth century. Of Shirazi (q.v.) descent, they appear to have been sunni Muslims who were fleeing shi'ite persecution in Persia. Also known as Djoumbe, they established the first sultanates on the island. The Almasela (q.v.), of Arabic descent, arrived in the seventeenth century. They appear to have been from Southern Arabia, and they claimed direct descent from the Prophet Mohammed through his daughter Fatima. Shortly after their arrival in Nzwani, in the middle of the seventeenth century, a member of this group married the Almadua Queen Manaou Idarous. The daughter of this union, Halima II, became the first representative of the Almasela line to rule in Nzwani. Thus began what was to be several centuries of conflict between these two groups over the right to rule Nzwani. As the Almasela were generally based in Mutsamudu (q.v.) and the Almadua were based in Domoni (q.v.), the conflict was also played out as a conflict between these two port cities. During the eighteenth century the sultans (q.v.) of Nzwani extended their hegemony over Mwali (q.v.) and Mahoré (q.v.). They also intervened from time to time in the affairs of Ngazidja (q.v.) as well.

By the 1800s the different sultans of Nzwani were appealing both to the British and the French for assistance in their internal conflicts. The British were the most sympathetic to these appeals, probably due in part to their concern for maintaining a strategic position in the Mozambique Channel and in part to balance the French presence in Mahoré. A British consulate was thus established in Nzwani in 1849. It was staffed first by Josiah Napier (until he died in 1851) and then by William Sunley (q.v.). Sunley got on well with Sultan Abdallah III (q.v.), established a plantation in the southwestern portion of the island, and rented slaves from the sultan in quantity. He resigned his post in 1867, after the British goverment objected to his operating a plantation on the island. In 1886 Sultan Abdallah III, facing a number of political and social difficulties, appealed to France for protection. Nzwani thus became a protectorate of France. A rebellion of slaves on the island in 1891 resulted in the takeover of the citadel in Mutsamudu, the sacking of the ancient capital of Domoni (q.v.), and the presence of French troops on the island. In 1909 Nzwani was officially ceded to France by Saïd Omar and the island was formally annexed.

-O-

OPPOSITION UNIE [United Opposition]. An unofficial grouping during the 1980s of former ministers and deputies in the Comoros who were opposed to the Ahmed Abdallah (q.v.) government. They were led by ex-Prime Minister Ali Mroudjae and included several other WaNgazidja such as Ahmed Abdou, Ali Bazi Selim, and Saïd Hassan Saïd Hachim. Most of this group were seen at one time as potential successors to Ahmed Abdallah (q.v.).

ORGANIZATION OF AFRICAN UNITY (OAU). The Comoros are a member of the Organization of African Unity and have attempted to plead there for the reintegration of Mahoré (q.v.) into the Federal Islamic Republic of the Comoro Islands. In response, the OAU has condemned France's occupation of Mahoré. It should also be noted that the Comoros were forbidden to attend the OAU conference of 1978 due to the presence of mercenaries (q.v.) in the islands at that time.

OUANI see WANI

P-Q

PAMANDZI. A satellite islet of the island of Mahoré (q.v.) and the site of the principal administrative offices of the Comoros between 1946 and 1962. There are three small cities, Dzaoudzi, Sandangue, and Labattoir, and a small lake, Dziana Dzaha, on Pamandzi Islet. The town of Dzaoudzi is located on a rocky outcrop linked to the islet by a mile-long dike. Pamandzi is also the current site of the Mahoré airport. In 1946, after World War II, France began to separate the Comoros administratively from Madagascar. The Comoros were designated an Overseas Territory of France and were placed under the authority of the High Commissioner of Madagascar. Pamandzi was chosen as a local administrative site for the Comoros, and a General Council was established with headquarters there. In 1952 the General Council was transformed into a Territorial Assembly, and in 1956 a Government Council was established, with administrative offices in Dzaoudzi. In 1959 the Territorial Assembly transferred its offices to Moroni (q.v.), becoming a Chamber of Deputies in 1961. The remaining administrative offices moved to Moroni in 1962, after the Comoros were granted separate administrative status from Madagascar.

PARTI POUR L'ÉVOLUTION DES COMORES (PEC) [Party for the Evolution of the Comoros]. A political party formed in 1972 in Moroni (q.v.).

PARTI POUR L'INDÉPENDANCE ET L'UNITÉ DES CO-MORES (PUIC) [Party for Unity and Independence for the Comoros]. In 1973 the Union Démocratique des Comores (q.v.) and the Rassemblement Démocratique des Peuples Comoriens (q.v.) merged to form the PUIC.

PARTI SOCIAL DÉMOCRATIQUE DES COMORES (PSDC) [Social Democratic Party of the Comoros]. A branch of the Rassemblement Démocratique des Peuples Comoriens (q.v.), or "white party" founded in Nzwani (q.v.) under the leadership of Ali Mirghane.

PARTI SOCIALISTE DES COMORES (PASOCO) [Socialist Party of the Comoros]. An early political party, PASOCO was formed in 1969. It was very active in the movement towards independence. By 1972 most political activists in the Comoros belonged to PASOCO.

PATSI (Patsy). An area of land east of the community of Mutsamudu (q.v.) on the island of Nzwani (q.v.). Patsi is named after the plantation founded and operated in the late nineteenth century by the American physician Benjamin F. Wilson (q.v.).

PIRATES. In the seventeenth and early eighteenth centuries the Comoro Islands were a haunt for the pirates who plagued the seafaring commerce of the western Indian Ocean. The islands were used for revictualizing, safe harbors, and jumping-off places to plunder the wealth of the western Indian Ocean. Prized targets of pirates were the ships of the East India trade, which passed through the Mozambique Channel on their way between India and Europe. The Comoros were ideally located for this purpose, in the northern end of the Mozambique Channel and halfway between eastern Africa and Madagascar, and offered protected anchorages, fresh water, fruit, and meat, as well as aid and companionship in some cases. The lagoon at Mahoré (q.v.) was a particularly common hideout for pirate ships. The pirates reputed to have been in the Comoros include Captain Quail, Captain Kidd, Captain North, Captain Thomas Harris, Captain Thomas Howard, John Ap Owen, Henry Every, William Ayre, William Cobb, and Davy Jones.

PLANTATIONS. Several early plantations were established by English, American, and French Colonials in the Comoros. Englishman William Sunley's (q.v.) Pomoni in southwestern Nzwani (q.v.) is probably the earliest of these. Patsi (q.v.), established by the American physician Benjamin Wilson (q.v.) in north-central Nzwani, was also established early. Once the French colonized the islands other colonial plantations developed rapidly. Bambao was established in 1893 in eastern Nzwani on Sultan Abdallah III's (q.v.) old land, and Nioumakele (q.v.) was established in 1900 in southern Nzwani. By 1907 more than two thirds of Nzwani had been turned into foreign-controlled plantations. Likewise, more than half of Ngazidja (q.v.) had been converted to plantations—primarily owned by the Société Anonyme de la Grande Comore (q.v.). Plantations on Mwali (q.v.) and Mahoré (q.v.) took up somewhat less of the total acreage of these islands. Fomboni (q.v.) and M'Remani were the principal plantations established on Mwali (some of these were also owned by Léon Humblot's [q.v.] company) while Dzoumogné, Soulou, and Kombani were the principal plantations on Mahoré (note that Kombani was also owned by Humblot). Sugar cane was one of the principal crops until the early 1900s, when sugar from beets became a major competitor on the world market. Other important plantation crops were copra (q.v.), vanilla (q.v.), cloves (q.v.), and ylang-ylang (q.v.).

POLITICAL PARTIES. The earliest political parties to form in the Comoros were the Rassemblement Démocratique des Peuples Comoriens (RDPC) (q.v.) and the Union Démocratique des Comores (UDC) (q.v.). Both were formed in 1968. The RDPC, formed by Saïd Mohamed Djaffar (q.v.), became known as the "white party" because candidates' names were placed on white ballots during elections. It was based primarily on Ngazidja (q.v.) but an allied group, the Parti Social Démocratique des Comores (PSDC) (q.v.) was also formed on Nzwani (q.v.). The UDC was known as the "green party" because candidates' names were placed on green ballots. It was primarily based in Nzwani. The Partie Socialiste des Comores (PASOCO) was formed in 1969, and UMMA (The People) (q.v.) was formed in 1971. While PASOCO was very active in the movement towards independence, UMMA advocated independence (q.v.) only with France's consent. By 1972 most political activists in the Comoros belonged to PASOCO. UMMA, however, is the party which eventually came under the control of Ali Soilih (q.v.). In 1972 the Parti pour l'Évolution des Comores (PEC) (q.v.) was formed and in 1973 the UDC and RDPC ("green" and "white") parties merged to form the Parti pour l'Indépendance et l'Unité des Comores (PUIC) (q.v.). All political parties were outlawed between the years of 1978 and 1990, with the exception of the Union Comorienne pour le Progrès (UCP, also known as Udzima) (q.v.), the party of Ahmed Abdallah (q.v.). For 12 years this was the only political party that was officially permitted in the Comoros. Although it was Ahmed Abdallah's party, it was also the party of several unsuccessful opposition candidates for the presidency. Despite the ban, in 1984 Union pour une République Démocratique aux Comores (URDC) (q.v.), a party in exile, was formed in Paris by Abdallah Mouazoir (q.v.). The multiparty system was reinstated in 1990 by President Saïd Mohamed Djohar (q.v.). Since 1990, several different political parties have developed in the Comoros, including CHUMA (Fraternity and Unity Party), Mouvement Démocratique Populaire (MDP), Mouvement pour la Rénovation et l'Action Démocratique (q.v.) (MOURAD), Parti Comorien pour la Démocratie et le Progrès (PCDP), Rassemblement pour le Changement et la Démocratie (RACHADE) (q.v.), Union Comorienne pour le Progrès, Union Nationale pour la Démocratie aux Comores (UNDC) and Uwezo (formerly Union pour une République Démocratique aux Comores or URDC).

POLYGYNY. A form of polygamy in which a man is permitted to have two or more wives at the same time. Following Islamic law, Comorian men can marry only up to four wives simultaneously and are expected to treat each wife equally. This practice is combined with matrilocality (q.v.), a pattern of marriage (q.v.) residence in which the married couple resides with the wife's family. When a man marries more than one wife, consequently, his wives live in separate house-holds, and the husband spends equal time visiting each wife. As in most societies where polygyny is practiced, fewer than 50% of the married men in the Comoros have more than one wife. (See also FAMILY)

POMONI RIVER. This river runs in a southwesterly direction from the center of Nzwani (q.v.), passing through the coastal town of Pomoni as it exits to the sea.

POPULATION. The Comoros are one of the most densely popu-lated areas of Africa, and population is increasing rapidly. In December 1986 the population of the entire archipelago was officially estimated to be 484,000 persons. The 1980 census, which did not include Mahoré (q.v.), indicated 335,150 (167,089 males, 168,061 females); the population of Mahoré was estimated as 50,740. More recent estimates suggest an overall total of 470,000: 210,000 on Ngazidja (q.v.), 200,000 on Nzwani (q.v.), 40,000 on Mahoré, and 20,000 on Mwali (q.v.). This would place average popula-tion density slightly over 544 per square mile. Density is lowest in Mwali (approximately 370) and highest in Nzwani (approximately 1,280 per square mile). In 1980 these figures were considerably less, with an average of 470 persons per square mile ($900/m^2$ on Nzwani and $170/m^2$ on Mwali). At least 27% of the population now lives in urban areas. The present rate of population increase is estimated at 3.5% per year with an annual birth rate of 47 per 1,000 and an annual death rate of 12 per 1,000. A recent estimate of the fertility rate is 6.8 births per woman. Life expectancy at birth is 59 years for females and 54 years for males. Population projec-tions indicate the possibility of a population of 700,000 to 800,000 by the year 2000 and a population density of 800 to 900 per square mile. (See also ETHNICITY.)

PORTS. The traditional ports of the Comoros were shallow-water landing spots protected by natural promontories or con-structed docks extending into the ocean. These were suffi-cient for the Arab-style dhows and the European sailing ships that plied the trade routes in the Indian Ocean prior to the 1900s. Principal ports were Moroni (q.v.) in Ngazidja (q.v.); Mutsamudu (q.v.) and Domoni (q.v.) in Nzwani (q.v.); and the lagoon area of Mahoré (q.v.). More recently, with financial aid from several Arab nations, a deep-water port has been constructed at Mutsamudu (q.v.) which can serve today's deeper draft ships.

PORTUGUESE. The Portuguese first visited the islands in approximately 1500. Linguistic evidence suggests that contact was long enough or intensive enough to result in some word-borrowing into Comorian languages (q.v.). Words such as *meza* (from mesa, table), *zeti* (from azeite, oil), and *bas* (from basta, stop) are examples. In addition several card games (q.v.) and the words for playing cards appear also to have been borrowed from the Portuguese.

PREHISTORY see ARCHAEOLOGY

PRODUCTS see EXPORTS

QADIRIYA see TARIQA

-R-

RADIO. Radio Comores broadcasts programs in French, Arabic, and Comorian languages (q.v.). It has owned its own transmitters since 1959.

RAINFALL. Rainfall varies from island to island and from season to season. One generally refers to rainy and dry seasons. From December to April (rainy season) rainfall is abundant on all four islands. There may even be severe storms in January and February. From May to November (dry season) there is significantly less rainfall. Occasionally this dry period is broken by brief rains in August or September. From island to island specific microclimates also influence the overall amount of rain in a given area, with more rain on the west coasts of the islands, on the high plateaus and at higher altitudes in general. (See also CLIMATE.)

RAMANATAKA. Sultan of Mwali (q.v.) from 1828 until his death in 1842. A Merina general, Ramanataka was the brother-in-law of the Malagasy king Radama I and had assisted in conquering the Sakalava coast. A change in Malagasy politics resulted in his fleeing that island in 1826. Abdallah II (q.v.), Sultan of Nzwani (q.v.), provided asylum for Ramanataka in Nzwani and in 1828 Ramanataka and his soldiers assisted in the establishment of Nzwani domination over Mwali. He then moved his family and soldiers to Mwali and became sultan of that island. He was involved in politics in each of the other islands, responding to requests for assistance from Ngazidja (q.v.), fighting against the Sakalava (q.v.) in Mahoré (q.v.), and meddling in the politics of the sultanate of Nzwani. As sultan of Mwali he converted to Islam, changed his name to Abderrahman, and reached out to Zanzibar (q.v.) for assistance. Shortly before his death he indicated his desire to have his young daughter, Djoumbe Fatima (q.v.), succeed him as ruler of Mwali, and advised her to rely on France for protection.

RASSEMBLEMENT DÉMOCRATIQUE DES PEUPLES CO-MORIENS (RDPC) [Democratic Assembly of the Comorian People]. An early political party, formed in 1968. Based primarily on Ngazidja (q.v.) it was later known as the "white party" because candidates' names were placed on white ballots during elections.

RASSEMBLEMENT POUR LE CHANGEMENT ET LA DÉMOCRATIE (RACHADE) [Organization for Change and Democracy]. A political party formed in 1991, soon after President Saïd Mohamed Djohar (q.v.) reinstated a multiparty system.

RELIGION. The principal religion practiced in the Comoros is the Shafi'i rite of Sunni Islam. Five brotherhoods are differentiated. Non-Islamic religious practices include a form of eel worship in Nzwani (q.v.) and a form of spirit possession/healing ceremony practiced primarily by women (q.v.). (See also ISLAM; RITUALS.)

RIFAIYA see TARIQA

RITUALS. In addition to Islamic rituals, there are also numerous agrarian and local rituals peculiar to specific locations in the Comoros. These include collective year-end sacrificial meals, seasonal games (q.v.), bull-runs and boxing matches, spirit possession and healing ceremonies, eel-feeding in sacred places, and blood-letting in cases of first catches. Many of these rituals are supervised by religious practitioners known locally as *mwalimu,* who are adept in contacting the local spirits or djinns and ascertaining their needs and desires. Many of these are examples of reinterpretations of African observances (eels substituting for snakes, for example) and many have been Islamized to some degree as well (sacrificing a goat in conjunction with observance of Islamic new year, for example). (See also RELIGION.)

RIVERS. Ngazidja (q.v.) has no permanent rivers. Nzwani (q.v.), Mwali (q.v.), and Mahoré (q.v.), however, are drained by a network of more or less permanent rivers and streams. Approximately 40 rivers in Nzwani descend from the high plateaus. Some flow through deep gorges and canyons and create spectacular waterfalls. Most notable are the Ajaho, Jomani, Tatenga (q.v.), and those of the towns of Pomoni and Mutsamudu (q.v.). Mwali's (q.v.) rivers begin about a hundred feet below the crater line and run through deep valleys. Most notable are those of the towns of Drondoni-Foungui, Fomboni (q.v.), and Onombeni. Rivers in Mahoré are generally slow-moving and meandering. Most notable are those of the towns of Kwale and Kaweni. (See also GEOLOGY.)

-S-

SABENAS. Name colloquially used for Comorians who fled the Majunga (q.v.) massacre of 1977. Over the span of several generations a large colony of Comorians had become established in Majunga, on the northwest coast of Madagascar. Shopkeepers, restaurant owners, and entrepreneurs of every type, they had come to represent a wealthy class of business people. As such, they became a target for the anti-Comorian massacres of 1977. No amount of assimilation or acculturation was sufficient to protect them. Many survivors were evacuated to the Comoros on Air Sabena airplanes. As a result they are now sometimes now referred to as "Sabenas" in the Comoros. The word is also occasionally extended to any Comorian who is from Madagascar or who speaks with a Malagasy accent or dresses in a Malagasy style. Resettled primarily in port cities in the Comoros—Moroni (q.v.), Mutsamudu (q.v.), Dzaoudzi, Fomboni (q.v.), and Domoni (q.v.)—they have swelled the urban population of the islands significantly. Many have opened small shops, and others have become specialists in electronic and mechanical repairs. To the extent that they retain customs acquired in Madagascar, or continue to speak Malagasy, they seem to be regarded as outsiders rather than as Comorians. (See also MAJUNGA.)

SAID ALI, SULTAN. Sultan of Bambao, Ngazidja (q.v.), from 1875 until 1912 when he ceded the island to the French. Saïd Ali had received a French eduction in Mahoré (q.v.) and was receptive to French assistance in his quest for control over the entire island. In 1883 Saïd Ali granted a commercial concession to Léon Humblot (q.v.), a French naturalist. An agreement between the two men gave Humblot ownership of any land he wished to cultivate and promised the return of 10% of any profits to Saïd Ali. Despite protest from the other sultans of Ngazidja, France established a protectorate over the island and installed a resident with Saïd Ali's assistance. Local resistance to Saïd Ali and the French continued, however, and by 1893 Saïd Ali fled to Réunion. Still claiming to be overall Sultan of Ngazidja, in 1912 Saïd Ali sued Humblot for land, money, and a complete accounting of the finances of the Société Humblot (q.v.). After winning the suit, he abdicated as Sultan of Bambao, Ngazidja and ceded the island to France.

SAID IBRAHIM (PRINCE). Second President of the Territory of the Comoro Islands, from 1970 to 1972. The Government Council elected him President after the death of Saïd Mohamed Cheikh (q.v.) in 1970.

SAID MOHAMED CHEIKH. First President of the Territory of the Comoro Islands, from 1961 to 1970. He proposed the nationalization of non-cultivated lands in 1946. In 1961, when the Comoros were given administrative autonomy and a Government Council was established, Saïd Mohamed Cheikh was elected as the first President of the Council. As President of the Council he was also recognized as President of the Territory and functioned as a deputy to the French National Assembly. Taking office in a period of internal autonomy in the 1960s, he led the Comoros in significant economic and social development. Roads were paved, and the number of schools and hospitals grew, in spite of the relative non-support of the Territory by France. The first lycée built in the Comoros, in Moroni (q.v.), was named for him. He died in 1970.

SAID MOHAMED DJAFFAR (PRINCE). Third Territorial President of the Comoro Islands, President of the Council of Government (and therefore of the Territory of the Comoros) for a brief period in 1972. After becoming President he publicly demanded independence from France, then resigned from office, thus precipitating an election. The election was won by Ahmed Abdallah (q.v.), leader of the Union Démocratique des Comores (q.v.).

SAID MOHAMED DJOHAR. Current President of the Comoro Islands. The half-brother of Ali Soilih (q.v.), Saïd Mohamed Djohar was the Chief Justice of the Supreme Court of the Comoro Islands when Ahmed Abdallah (q.v.) was assassinated. Constitutional mandate placed the Chief Justice first in line to replace the President until elections could be held. Saïd Mohamed Djohar therefore became interim President in November 1989. He was replaced briefly by mercenaries (q.v.) who attempted to seize power directly, but France and South Africa (q.v.) suspended aid and France intervened militarily in order to oust the mercenaries. He was then elected President in 1990 in two separate elections and France resumed its aid. (The first election was abandoned due to claims of fraud lodged by his opponent Mohamed Taki.) He has survived two coup attempts in 1990 and 1991, and one assassination attempt in 1994. He has reinstated a multiparty system, has granted amnesty to all political prisoners, has established diplomatic relations with the United States (q.v.), and has supervised the signing of a bilateral agreement with South Africa for Comorian development.

SAKALAVA. A Malagasy group with significant influence in the Comoros in the 1800s. In the late seventeenth century Sakalava chiefs conquered the northwest coast of Madagascar, took over the Islamic trading communities of the area, and become involved in trade with European powers in the Indian Ocean. Some of the trade was for slaves, and the Sakalava were able to provide such merchandise by means of a series of ongoing wars with plateau Merina that lasted through the eighteenth century. Towards the end of the eighteenth century, however, a new source for slaves became necessary, and the Sakalava, together with the Betsimisaraka, turned their attention to the Comoros. Raids on the Comoros probably began as early as the 1790s and lasted until the 1820s. They were carried out by fleets of large (about 30-foot-long) outrigger canoes. Conflict in the 1800s between the Sakalava, the Merina, and the Betsimisaraka extended to the Comoros. In the 1830s and 1840s, in particular, the conflict pitted Andriantsouli (q.v.), a Sakalava chief who had settled in Mahoré (q.v.), against Ramanataka (q.v.), a Merina chief who had settled in Nzwani (q.v.) and become the sultan of Mwali (q.v.). Also involved in these conflicts was Andrianavi, a Betsimisaraka chief from Madagascar who was attempting to invade Mahoré. Andriantsouli finally ceded Mahoré to the French in 1841, although he continued to maintain that he was its rigthful ruler. When he died in 1845 the Sakalava chiefs on Mahoré attempted to elect his son, Bangala, as ruler but the French refused to recognize him. The linguistic and cultural impact of the Sakalava can still be seen in present day Mahoré.

SALIM, SULTAN. Ruler of Nzwani (q.v.) between 1840 and 1855.

SCHOOLS see EDUCATION

SHADHILIYA see TARIQA

SHIRAZI. A group of migrants said to have founded several communities along the East African coast and the Comoro Islands and who are still revered and proudly thought of as ancestors by a number of people from various communities in the western Indian Ocean area. The legend of the Shirazi migration was noted by the Portuguese (q.v.) in the East African coastal community of Kilwa as early as the six-teenth century, and several versions have been collected since then. Although different in details the various ver-sions share the general outline of a migration by ship of a family originally from Shiraz in Persia. The father and leader of the group is said to have landed in the Comoro Islands on the island of Nzwani (q.v.). The legend on that island contends that the Shirazi founded several towns and constructed several mosques on Nzwani. One of these com-munities is Domoni (q.v.), the ancient capital of the island, where some inhabitants today proudly claim descent from the Shirazi and have named the local soccer team after them. The legend also relates that 40 years after the arrival of the Shirazi on Nzwani a quarrel among the leader's sons led to their dispersal and the subsequent founding of com-munities in Mahoré (q.v.), Madagascar, and the East African coast. While there is some question about the de-tails of the legend, the general notion of a migration of an influential group of people who had some ties to the ancient trading center of Shiraz is undoubtedly true. Most likely is that a prominent group of people from a trading community on the northwestern shore of the Indian Ocean migrated by ship to the Comoro Islands at some time before the end of the twelfth century and founded or were responsible for the expansion of several communities. This is consistent with the archaeological and historical evidence concerning the Shirazi from the East African coast as well as in the Comoro Islands.

SHIROMANI. A large red-and-white cloth which is draped about the body and used as a privacy veil by women (q.v.) in Nzwani when they go out in public. Under the Ali Soilih (q.v.) government women were forbidden to wear the *shiro-mani*. *Ziromani* (pl.) were collected and publicly burned in an effort to "modernize" women's public image. Although this was disruptive to many older women, the younger women adjusted fairly well to the new exposure. After the Soilih regime ended, many older women returned to the comfort and privacy of the *shiromani*. Younger women use the *shiromani* as an outer garb but rarely veil their faces with it.

SHUFELDT, COMMODORE ROBERT W. An American naval officer who commanded the *USS Ticonderoga* on a visit to African waters in the late eighteenth century. He arrived at Nzwani in 1879. Commodore Shufeldt signed a treaty with Sultan Abdallah III (q.v.), the ruler of the island, that guaranteed most-favored-nation status for the United States (q.v.), established the right of American citizens to reside and own property on the island, pledged protection for United States' ships and crews, and proclaimed the right of extraterritoriality for all Americans residing on Nzwani. The treaty was submitted to the United States Senate in March of 1880 by President Hayes, but no action was taken.

SISAL. Fiber made from the leaves of the agave plant used in making rope. Grown mainly in Nzwani, (q.v.), it was an important export until the mid-1950s. After that exports (q.v.) fell off due to low world prices. The Comoros ceased exporting sisal in 1971.

SOCIÉTÉ ANONYME DE LA GRANDE COMORE (SAGC) [The Grande Comore Company]. Begun in 1885 as the Société Humblot, the SAGC resulted from an agreement between Léon Humblot (q.v.) and Sultan Saïd Ali (q.v.). The first concession of land from Saïd Ali to Humblot was supplemented by Humblot until, in 1909, he owned 52,000 hectares—more than half of Ngazidja (q.v.)—which included several villages whose populations were thus enslaved to work on the Humblot plantations. In 1909 Humblot purchased an additional 5,000 hectares in Mwali (q.v.). After Humblot's death the SAGC began losing land to competing plantation companies. In 1938 it was taken over by the Société Colonial de Bambao (q.v.) of Nzwani (q.v.).

SOCIÉTÉ COLONIAL DE BAMBAO (SCB) [The Bambao Company]. A large plantation company established in Nzwani (q.v.), in 1893, by two French planters named Bouin and Tegouin who had gained control of Sultan Abdallah III's (q.v.) property, in the eastern part of the island. Together with the French perfumer Chiris they created the Société Colonial de Bambao there. Eventually known as the SCB or even more commonly as the Société Bambao, the company continued to grow and to absorb other holdings in Nzwani. In 1921 it absorbed Patsi (q.v.) to the north. In 1923 it acquired Pomoni to the southwest. By 1961 the Société Bambao controlled approximately half of the arable land in Nzwani. The Société Bambao also expanded its holdings to other islands. In 1924 it purchased the old Lambert concession on Mwali from the Société Humblot (q.v.). Then in 1938 it gained control of the entire Société Humblot holdings. This meant that the Société Bambao now controlled more than half of the land area of Ngazidja (q.v.) as well as that of Nzwani. In 1948 the Société Bambao acquired the Dzumonye plantation in northern Mahoré (q.v.), thus giving it control over land in all four islands. (See also SOCIÉTÉ ANONYME DE LA GRANDE COMORE.)

SOCIÉTÉ HUMBLOT see SOCIÉTÉ ANONYME DE LA GRANDE COMORE; also HUMBLOT, LÉON

SOCIÉTÉ POUR LE DÉVELOPPEMENT ÉCONOMIQUE DES COMORES (SODEC) [Society for the Economic Development of the Comoros]. This is the agency through which the French initiated research and development programs in the territory of the Comoros during the colonial period.

SOUTH AFRICA. Following the reinstatement of the Ahmed Abdallah (q.v.) government in 1978, relations with South Africa improved significantly. Many tourists in the Comoros are now from South Africa. Hotels (q.v.) have been built on

Ngazidja (q.v.), Nzwani (q.v.), and Mwali (q.v.) with the assistance of Nouvelle Socotel, a South African-led consortium with government interest, and it is possible to fly directly to the Comoros from Johannesburg. Twelve thousand tourists from South Africa were estimated for 1988 (as compared to two thousand just two years earlier). There is some indication that the mercenary forces that had been maintained in the Comoros by Ahmed Abdallah were partially financed by South Africa. Other accusations have included the possibility that mercenaries (q.v.) in the Comoros served as a link between South Africa and RENAMO rebels in Mozambique, or between South Africa and Iran.

SULTANS. Until their occupation by the French in the late 1800s and early 1900s, the Comoros had been ruled by generations of Sultans and their families. The passage of power was generally from father to son within families but occasionally it was a brother, daughter, nephew or niece who would inherit (or seize) power from the ruling sultan. Each island had one or more sultans, and relationships among them varied from cordial and cooperative to hostile and warring. Each sultan's base of power was generally one of the urban centers of an island. On the island of Nzwani (q.v.), for example, both Domoni (q.v.) and Mutsamudu (q.v.) were ruled by sultans and palaces were built in both of these towns. In the 1800s the French were able to take advantage of conflicts between and among individual sultans in order to occupy and colonize the islands.

SUNLEY, WILLIAM. A nineteenth-century representative of Britain in the Comoros. To reinforce its influence in the Mozambique Channel and to counterbalance the installation of the French in Mahoré (q.v.), the British government established a consulate at Mutsamudu (q.v.) in 1849. Josiah Napier, the first consul, died in 1851 and was replaced by William Sunley, a navigator from Bournemouth. While serving as consul Sunley established a plantation at Pomoni where he employed slaves rented from Sultan Abdallah III (q.v.). By 1865 more than 600 slaves were working on this plantation. The situation was to prove an embarrassment to Britain, which was attempting to repress the slave trade at that time. After a visit by David Livingston, Sunley was offered a choice: give up the plantation or give up his position as consul. He chose to keep the plantation and was removed from foreign service in 1867.

-T-

TARIQA. An Arabic term meaning "road, way, or path," it refers to the Muslim religious orders or brotherhoods that have embraced mysticism as a path to true faith. Each was founded by a saint whose memory is revered, and each has adopted a specific rite for contact with Allah. The Shadhiliya, Rifaiya, and Qadiriya orders have numerous followers in the Comoros today.

TATENGA. A major river of Nzwani (q.v.), Tatenga runs in an easterly direction from the central highlands of Nzwani. It exits to the sea to the north of the town of Bambao. Tatenga has a very steep long-drop waterfall near Bambao and a small deep pool which has become a popular swimming spot for area residents. The river has been used as a private source of hydroelectric power by the Société Colonial de Bambao (q.v.).

TELECOMMUNICATIONS AND POSTAL SERVICES. Inter-island telephone communications rely primarily on radio and telegraph. International telephone communications rely on a one-way radio link with Antanarivo and two-way radio links with Paris. There is much greater demand for telephone connections than there are connections available. There are few exchanges and only a few hundred individuals and companies have telephones. There are plans to install a VHF network for inter-island communications and long-term plans to install an earth station to receive satellite transmissions. Nine post offices handle mail and money order transactions: four on Ngazidja (q.v.), two each on Nzwani (q.v.) and Mahoré (q.v.), and one on Mwali (q.v.).

TERRITOIRE D'OUTRE-MER (TOM) [Overseas territory]. In 1946 the Comoros were declared to be a TOM of France and an elected general council was established, to be presided over by a president who would report to the high commissioner in Madagascar.

TIME. The Comoros are situated at Greenwich Mean Time plus three hours. The proximity of the islands to the equator makes the days and nights relatively even throughout the year, and at least two local time systems are in use which count the first hour of the day as sunrise (approximately six a.m.) and the first hour of the night as sunset (approximately six p.m.) The European midnight-and-noon-based time system is also used, especially in urban areas.

TOURISM. The Comoros have always been attractive to tourists and tourism has become an important part of the local economy. A significant boost to the islands' attractiveness to tourists was provided in 1987 when the Comoro government concluded an agreement with South African (q.v.) authorities to construct and refurbish hotels (q.v.) on the islands. There are now twelve hotels and numerous small guest houses in the islands. Restaurants have also been constructed. Direct connections with South Africa, Kenya, Tanzania, Madagascar, and France have also helped to stimulate the tourist trade. Most tourists have been from Europe and South Africa, but there is an increasing number of visitors from Arab countries (q.v.). As the Comoros are still somewhat off of the beaten path it is the more affluent tourists who have been attracted to the islands. With its tropical climate, interesting old towns, and varied marine fauna, the Comoros are likely to continue to develop significant interest as a tourist destination in the future.

TRADE AND COMMERCE see ECONOMY; EXPORTS; IMPORTS

TRANSPORTATION. Transportation between and within the islands is not easy. Traditionally Arab-style sailing ships transported individuals between the islands. More recently air transport has facilitated inter-island travel. Travel within each island has been hampered by the rugged terrain, particularly on Nzwani (q.v.) with its central peak and three mountainous spines. Nevertheless, there is much inter-island and intra-island travel. Most of the seaports in the Comoros are shallow ports accommodating the traditional Indian Ocean craft. European style boats, requiring deeper ports, traditionally have anchored offshore in Moroni (q.v.) for unloading by smaller dhows, or unloaded their goods in Madagascar, Mombasa, Dar es Salaam, or Réunion for transshipment to the Comoros in smaller boats or by air.

As a result early emphasis was put on developing air connections to and within the Comoros. Each island has a small airport, and Ngazidja (q.v.) also has a large international airport, Hahaia (q.v.), which was recently built to accommodate jumbo jet aircraft. Most essential oils and spices are exported by air. Imported fresh meats and vegetables also arrive by air. Individual travel between islands is generally by air, even though it is more expensive than travel by sea.

Most inter-island transport of cargo is by sea. Recently an international deep-water harbor was constructed in Mutsamudu (q.v.), Nzwani, and it is planned for this to become the international seaport for the Comoros. The government has assisted several maritime companies (e.g., Société Comorienne de Navigation, Comoros National Shipping Company) in developing localized ocean transport capabilities, and at least four international shipping companies have established links with the Comoros.

The road system built by the colonial French was a network of roads extending outward from the principal ports or airports on each island and serving the principal coastal areas in which export crops were grown. For the most part, these were coastal ring roads. On Nzwani the road from the port city of Mutsamudu to the plantation areas of Bambao and Domoni (q.v.) must traverse at least one of the mountanous spines of the island. Although many of the major roads are paved, feeder roads to the interior villages and plateaus are generally unpaved or consist of foot paths and trails. Many small farmers from the interior must walk to the coastal towns to sell their produce or handicrafts and to purchase imported goods and fish (q.v.). Since the 1970s much effort has gone into expanding the network of main roads and feeder roads. None of the rivers (q.v.) are navigable. (See also PORTS.)

TROU DE PROPHÈTE [The Prophet's Hole]. Also known as le Lac Salée, or the Salt Lake. Located near Bangoi-Kouni near the northern end of Ngazidja (q.v.), this lake's saltiness is said to result from an underground connection with the sea. Oral tradition has it that a foreign traveller was once refused the hospitality of a village. On his departure the earth opened and swallowed the town and its inhabitants. It is said that the town's remains can be found in the depths of this salt lake.

-U-

UDZIMA see UNION COMORIENNE POUR LE PROGRÈS

UHURU [Freedom]. A mimeographed newspaper produced during the 1970s by the Parti Socialiste des Comores (q.v.). Approximately 500 copies were distributed each week. It featured articles on current affairs, Marxist analyses of the society and economy of the islands, and gossip and criticism aimed at public officials. It advocated independence (q.v.), self-help, and the dissolution of what it saw as traditional impediments to progress, such as the Grand Marriage.

UMMA [The People]. A political party formed in 1971, advocating independence (q.v.) only with France's consent. This is the party which eventually came under the control of Ali Soilih (q.v.).

UNION COMORIENNE POUR LE PROGRÈS (UCP, also Udzima [Unity]) [Comorian Union for Progress]. When party politics was banned between 1978 and 1990, this was the only political party that was officially permitted in the Comoros. The party of Ahmed Abdallah (q.v.) during those years, UCP was also the party of several unsuccessful opposition candidates for the presidency.

UNION DÉMOCRATIQUE DES COMORES (UDC) [Democratic Union of the Comoros]. An early political party, formed in 1968. Based primarily in Nzwani (q.v.), UDC became known as the "green party" because candidates' names were placed on green ballots during elections.

UNION POUR UNE RÉPUBLIQUE DÉMOCRATIQUE AUX COMORES (URDC) [Union for a Democratic Republic in the Comoros]. A party founded in 1984 in Paris by Abdallah Mouazoir (q.v.), Ali Soilih's (q.v.) former foreign minister. In 1990, after Saïd Mohamed Djohar (q.v.) reinstated a multiparty system, URDC was reorganized and renamed Uwezo (Leadership).

UNITED NATIONS. The Comoros were admitted into the United Nations in November 1975, shortly after independence (q.v.).

UNITED STATES. There have been informal relationships between the United States and the Comoro archipelago at least since the middle 1800s and possibly earlier. It is also possible that Comorian slaves were taken to the United States in the early 1800s. In those years the Comoros were a common stopping place for American whaling ships (q.v.) seeking to reprovision their stores of livestock and fresh water. Some two dozen American whaling ships are estimated to have stopped in the Comoros each year during the 1850s. From time to time individuals from those ships would decide to stay on in the Comoros rather than to continue with the ship.

One of these was Benjamin Wilson (q.v.), an American physician from New Bedford, Massachusetts. Wilson was the physician on a whaling ship which had stopped in the Comoros when he decided to remain on Nzwani (q.v.), in 1871. Settling on land to the east of Mutsamudu (q.v.), he established a plantation named Patsi (q.v.) on 1,500 acres of land leased to him by Sultan Abdallah III (q.v.). In addition he became Abdallah III's private physician. To this day Wilson and his plantation are well-remembered in the oral history of the island. Sultan Abdallah III also attempted to develop more formal relations with the United States and in 1879, a few years after Wilson settled in Nzwani, he signed a treaty with Commander Robert Shufeldt (q.v.), of the *USS Ticonderoga,* guaranteeing most-favored-nation status for the United States, establishing the right of American citizens to reside and own property on the island, pledging protection for US ships and crews, and proclaiming the right of extraterritoriality for all Americans residing on Nzwani. Although the treaty was submitted to the United States Senate in March of 1880 by President Hayes, no action was taken.

After the French took possession of the archipelago there was little or no additional formal contact between the Comoros and the United States until trading relations were established in the 1970s. The Comoros then began exporting vanilla (q.v.) and essential oils to the United States. Recently, with new American laws requiring labeling of all ingredients and a general trend in the US towards natural ingredients of all kinds, the United States has become one of the largest importers of Comorian vanilla. Today, young Comorians travel to the US on business and increasing numbers choose to pursue their higher education in this country. The US and the Soviet Union experimented for a time, during the 1970s and 1980s, with the idea of being prepared to use the western Indian ocean region as a cold-war theatre, and each had several warships in the Mozambique channel as well as in the Indian Ocean in general. The current president of the Comoros, Saïd Mohamed Djohar (q.v.), has established diplomatic relations with the United States, and there are currently several US Peace Corps Volunteers working in the Comoros.

UWEZO see UNION POUR UNE RÉPUBLIQUE DÉMOCRA-TIQUE AUX COMORES

-V-

VANILLA (*Vanilla fragrans*). Of Central American origin, vanilla has been widely introduced in tropical regions such as the Comoros. Vanilla was introduced into the Comoros from Nossi-Be in Madagascar in 1873. Today the Comoros are second only to Madagascar in world production and export of vanilla, producing nearly 200 tons annually (as compared to 1,000 tons in Madagascar). Vanilla accounts for nearly 30% of all Comorian exports (q.v.), second only to ylang-ylang (q.v.) as a major export crop. It is particularly important in Ngazidja (q.v.), accounting for over half of that island's export earnings. 80% of the Comoros' vanilla exports are grown on Ngazidja. Vanilla vines are mostly grown interspersed with food crops such as maize, cassava, and rice, and in the shade of coconut (q.v.) and other trees. Planting and weeding begin the season, usually in September, and flowers must be pollinated by hand, thus making the production of vanilla a labor-intensive operation. The pods are picked during the cool dry season, between July and September, and then processed, dried, and prepared for export. About five pounds of green vanilla produces one pound of dried vanilla. Vanilla is cultivated almost entirely by individual farmers and processed by family and cooperative preparers. The development of vanillin, an artificial vanilla substitute, in the 1950s temporarily depressed the market for natural vanilla. More recently the market has improved, thanks in part to the efforts of Univanille, a producers' organization including the Comoros, Madagascar, and Réunion which has been actively promoting natural vanilla. Laws requiring labeling of ingredients in the United States (q.v.) and Europe and a general trend in these regions towards natural ingredients of all kinds has also helped the market for natural vanilla. The US is one of the principal importers of Comorian vanilla.

VOLCANOS. Although all of the islands were initially formed by volcanos, only one volcano, Karthala (q.v.), is currently active.

-W-

WANI. An old walled town on the northern shore on Nzwani (q.v.), on the bay just to the east of Mutsamudu (q.v.), Wani is also the site of Nzwani's airport. Wani has a population of approximately 7,000 and is rapidly becoming seen as an eastern suburb of Mutsamudu. Attacked by Malagasy slave raiders in the late eighteenth century, it is said to have been one of the towns in which the upper class Islamic families of the islands lived and owned land. Traditional indigenous pottery was still being manufactured in Wani in the 1970s.

WHALING SHIPS. In the 1800s the Comoros were a common stopping place for American whaling ships. As other international trading ships had discovered, the Comoros were an excellent place in which to restock fresh water and other provisions. Approximately two dozen American whaling ships per year are estimated to have stopped in the Comoros between the years of 1852 and 1858 alone.

WHITE PARTY see RASSEMBLEMENT DÉMOCRATIQUE DES PEUPLES COMORIENS

WILSON, BENJAMIN F., DR. An American Doctor from New Bedford, Massachussetts, who settled on Nzwani (q.v.) in 1871, served as private doctor to Sultan Abdallah III (q.v.), and established a successful plantation of 1,500 acres on the island. The land for the plantation was granted to him by Sultan Abdallah III (q.v.), for 30 years, at an annual rent of 200 piasters. Wilson named the plantation Patsi (q.v.) and the area east of Mutsamudu (q.v.) where the plantation was located, is still known by that name today.

WOMEN. Women's status in the Comoros is a complex matter. Under Islamic law women's privacy is an important consideration, and this is borne out in the wearing of the privacy veil, the *shiromani* (q.v.) or *buibui* (q.v.), and in patterns of prayer, where women are generally provided with screened-off sections of the mosques in which to pray. Under the Ali Soilih (q.v.) presidency an effort was made to "modernize" women and their status. Women were forbidden to wear the privacy veils and were forced to make speeches in public squares. Although this was stressful to many older women, the younger women adjusted fairly well to the new exposure. After the Soilih presidency ended, many older women returned to the comfort and privacy of the *shiromani*. Younger women use the *shiromani* as an outer garment but rarely veil their faces with it. Many women still also prefer to eat separately from men, but will join the men at a meal if guests are invited.

In addition to their participation in Islam, many women also participate in spirit-possession cults and in Nzwani (q.v.) may bring offerings and requests to the sacred eels at Papani. Women also function as herbal doctors in their communities, and some claim contact with spirit advisors in medicinal matters. Both patrilineage and matrilineage are of importance in the Comoros. Women inherit and own land, houses, and personal items such as jewelry. In precolonial days women were the principal wealth-holders, functioning as bankers, lending funds to their husbands and brothers for commercial ventures abroad, and maintaining stores of trade goods. Today women provide men with assistance in establishing cash crop enterprises. Some women also operate small general stores or market produce. In this matrilocal and polygynous society, women are the social core and the economic base of the household and the community, relying on their male kin or on hired help for working the lands and bringing in harvests. Women are numbered among the precolonial sultans (q.v.) of the islands, particularly in Mwali (q.v.). These include Djoumbe Fatima (q.v.), Queen of Mwali between 1842 and 1878, and Sultan Halima, who ruled Nzwani briefly in the early 1800s. Although women still wield a significant amount of political influence today, it tends more often to be behind-the-scenes, rather than public, power.

WORLD BANK. The Comoros became a member of the World Bank in October 1976. To date two reports have been written by this organization on the Comoros.

Y-Z

YLANG-YLANG (*Cananga odorata*). A tree whose flower produces an oil that is extracted for export. The ylang-ylang tree was successfully introduced to the Comoros from Indonesia in the late 1800s. This large tree, with fragrant yellow flowers, is grown on all four islands. Tree branches are trained to grow low to the ground for ease in collecting the delicate flowers. The aromatic oil extracted from the flowers for export makes up the principal export of the Comoros. Although the tree will grow well on land which is not suitable for food crops, the quality of yields varies significantly with differences in soil quality. As a result Nzwani (q.v.), with its highly fertile soils, produces twice as much ylang-ylang essence as Ngazidja (q.v.), even though the number of trees on the two islands is similar. In the mid-1970s Nzwani exported 50 metric tons of ylang-ylang oil, Mahoré (q.v.) 21 metric tons, Ngazidja 19 metric tons, and Mwali (q.v.) 2 metric tons. Ylang-ylang oil makes up 35% of the total export income of the Comoros, and 75 to 95% of the world's oil of ylang-ylang is produced in the Comoros. The tree grows primarily in coastal areas below 1,600 feet and is grown by individual farmers as well as on large plantations (q.v.).

ZANZIBAR. The Islamic sultans (q.v.) of the Comoros maintained trading and political relations with Zanzibar from at least the sixteenth century. In the 1800s Zanzibar became involved in the politics of both Mwali (q.v.) and Ngazidja (q.v.). In Mwali, when Sultan Ramanataka (q.v.) converted to Islam, he reached out to Zanzibar for assistance. In 1851 his daughter, Djoumbe Fatima (q.v.), married a cousin of the sultan of Zanzibar. She entered into a protectorate with the sultan of Zanzibar in 1867. In Ngazidja, when Sultan Saïd Ali (q.v.) entered into an agreement with the French planter Léon Humblot (q.v.), several other Ngazidja sultans appealed to Zanzibar for assistance. In the 1900s Zanzibar was a particularly popular area for Comorian settlement, and by the 1960s was the site of a large expatriate Comorian mercantile community of approximately 30,000 Comorians. When anti-Comorian massacres erupted in Zanzibar in 1968, the remaining Comorians fled to the Comoros, settling primarily in the northern portions of Ngazidja.

SELECTED BIBLIOGRAPHY

INTRODUCTION

Travelers, traders, and scholars have written about the Comoro Islands for more than five hundred years. They have produced a body of literature that describes the physical conditions, history, people, and cultures of the archipelago, and there has been a substantial growth in this literature in recent times. Undoubtedly this increase in output has been the result of a mounting interest in affairs of countries surrounding the Indian Ocean in general and a recognition that the Comoro Islands occupy a strategic position in the western Indian Ocean area. This recent interest has drawn attention of scholars from a number of different countries to the Comoro Islands and there is also a growing literature by Comorian scholars trained in various disciplines and writing about their homeland. A quick glance at the bibliography, however, will reveal that the literature about the Comoros is predominantly French. This is due to France's political dominance for many years over the Islands.

Of the recent publications concerning the Comoro Islands the journal *Études Océan Indien* needs to be specially mentioned. First published in 1982 by the Institut National des Langues et Civilisations Orientales in Paris, this journal has become a major outlet for scholarship on historical, linguistic, and social data of the Comoros. It is now an indispensable resource for scholarly information on the islands. Another recent publication that may be of interest to some readers is *Jana na Leo*. It is primarily concerned with articles on social life of the island of Mahoré and is published in Mamoudzou, Mahoré.

This bibliography is not a complete listing of the works about the Comoro Islands. Theses and dissertations have been deliberately omitted from the bibliography since they are often very narrow in scope and difficult to obtain. Fictional works by Comorians, although they may be expressive of Comorian life or depict aspects of Comorian culture, have also been omitted from the bibliography because of the historical emphasis of the dictionary. Book reviews, international agency reports, government reports, and newspaper articles have also been omitted. Nonetheless, the bibliography provides a large number of materials written about the Comoro Islands. To assist the reader in consulting the bibliography the entries have been placed under the following subheadings:

> Bibliographies
> Economics
> General References
> Geography and Geology
> History and Archaeology
> Language
> Plants and Animals
> Culture and Society

Each of the above subdivisions contains entries alphabetized by author. The History and Archaeology section has been further subdivided into two separately alphabetized sections: (1) General Research and (2) Voyagers' Narratives. The comments by travellers from previous centuries have been separated out from the published archaeological and historical research. This organization is intended to make the bibliography a more useful primary reference.

BIBLIOGRAPHIES

Boulinier, Georges. Thèses et mémoires universitaires sur les Comores. *Journal des Africanistes* 49:173–177, 1979.

Dubins, Barbara. Nineteenth-century travel literature on the Comoro Islands: a bibliographical essay. *African Studies Bulletin* 12(2):138–146, 1969. ·

———. The Comoro Islands: a bibliographic essay. *African Studies Bulletin* 12(2):131–137, 1969.

Gorse, Jean. *Territoire des Comores bibliographie.* Paris: Bureau pour le Développément de la Production Agricole, 1964.

Grandidier, Alfred, G. Grandidier, et H. Froidevaux. *Collection des ouvrages anciens concernant Madagascar.* Paris: Comité de Madagascar, 1906–1920.

Lafon, Michel, Cheikh Moinaesha et Francis Jouannet. Bibliographie comorienne. Pp. 148–156 in Jouannet (ed.) *Des tons à l'accent, essai sur l'accentuation du comorien.* Univ. de Provence Aix-Marseille 1, 1989.

Witherell, J. C. *Madagascar and adjacent islands; a guide to official publications.* Washington: United States Government Printing Office, 1965.

ECONOMICS

Abdallah, Ahmed. La vanille et le cocotier, source de richesse des Comores. *Union française de Paris 87.* Paris, 1955.

Avignon, Marcel. Monographie de la Grande-Comore. *Bulletin*

Économique de Madagascar 18(4):239–241; 19(1):147–150; 19(3–4):161–164, 1921–22.

Bastian, G. La situation économique aux Comores. *Revue de géographie* 2:61–82, 1963.

Gaspart, Claude. The Comoro Islands since independence: an economic appraisal. *Proceedings of the International Conference on Indian Ocean Studies.* Perth, Australia, 1979.

Institut National de la Statistique et des Études Économiques. *Comptes économiques du territoire des Comores.* Paris, 1959–1961.

Poirier, Charles. Mayotte et dépendances (Première partie). *Bulletin Économique de Madagascar* 18(3):233–237, 1921.

Robineau, Claude. *Essai sur les phénomènes de comportment économique à Anjouan (Archipel des Comores).* Tananarive: Université de Madagascar, 1963.

World Bank Eastern African Regional Office. *The Comoros: current economic situation and prospects.* Washington: The World Bank, 1983.

——. *The Comoros: problems and prospects of a small, island economy.* Washington: The World Bank, 1979.

GENERAL REFERENCES

Alexander, Douglas. *Holiday in the islands: a guide to the Comores, Madagascar, Réunion and Rodrigues.* Capetown: Purnell, 1976.

Allen, Philip M. and John M. Ostheimer. Africa and the islands of the western Indian Ocean. *Munger Africana Library Notes* 35, 1976.

Augarde, G. *L'archipel des Comores.* Paris: CHEAM, 1951.

———. *Les îles Comores.* Paris: CHEAM, 1948.

Ballan, Philippe. Un probleme d'aujourd'hui: l'avenir des îles Comores. *Cahiers des ingenieurs agronomes* 211:33–36, 1966.

Barnds, W.J. Arms race or arms control in the indian ocean? *America* 127: 280–282, 1972.

Barraux, M. L'Auge de Sima. *Bulletin de l'Académie Malgache* 37:93–99, 1959.

Barraux, R. Les Iles Comores. *Revue Encyclopédique de l'Afrique* 4/5:22–26, 1962.

Bauer, M. Gesteinsproben der Wittu Insel, von Zanzibar, Archipel von den Comoren, Madagascar, Ceylon etc. Pp. 17–51 in Voeltzkow, A., *Reise in Ost-Afrika in den Jahren 1903–1905,* Bd. 1, Absteil II, 1911.

Berthiaux, Guy. *Introduction à l'étude des Comores.* Paris: CHEAM, 1947.

Blanchy, Sophie, Damir ben Ali et Saïd Moussa. *Guide des monouments historiques de la Grande Comore (Moroni, Ikoni, Itsandra-mdjini, Ntsudjini.)* Moroni: Editions du CNDRS, 1989.

Bosse, Auguste. La Grande Comore. *Revue coloniale* (2e partie) 8:120–127, 1846.

Bosse, Auguste and Pajot. La Grande-Comore. *Annales Maritimes: Sciences et Arts* (2e partie) 3:119–126, 1848.

Bossu-Picat, Christian. *Mayotte—Ile aux Parfums.* Paris: Editions Delroisse, n.d.

Bouchereau, A. Notes sur l'anthropologie de Madagascar, des

Comores et de la côte orientale d'Afrique. *L'Anthropologie* 8:149–164, 1897.

Bourde, André. The Comoro Islands: problems of a microcosm. *The Journal of Modern African Studies* 3(1):91–102, 1965.

Brolly, Mabe et Christain Vaisse. *Mayotte.* Editions du Pacifique, 1988.

C.E.E. *Renseignements de base concernant les departements d'outre-mer francais.* Bruxelles: Siege, 1962.

Chagnoux, Herve. Comores. *Revue Historique* 1983(544): 565–591, 1980.

Chagnoux, Herve and Ali Haribou. *Les Comores.* Paris: Presses Universitaires de France, 1980.

Cheikh, Mohammed Said. Les Comores dans l'Union Francaise. *Union Francaise et parlement* 21:29–40. Paris, 1951.

Colin, J. et E. Capmartin. Essai sur les Comores. Tome 13:129–170 dans *Annales des voyages de Malte-Brun.* Paris: Buison-Lemaire, 1810.

Comité de Défense des indigènes. *La Situation des indigè aux Comores.* Paris, 1904.

Cornu, H. *Paris et bourbon, La politique française dans l'Océan indien.* Paris: Académie des Sciences d'Outre-mer, 1984.

Cottrell, Alvin S. *Sea power and strategy in the Indian Ocean.* Beverly Hills: Sage Publications, 1981.

Cottrell, Alvin S. and R. M. Burrell (editors). *The Indian Ocean: its political, economic, and military importance.* New York: Praeger, 1972.

Couder, P. L'archipel des Comores. Dans *La France de l'Océan Indien.* Paris: Editions maritimes et coloniales, 1952.

Daddah, Yacoub Ould. Les îles au large de l'Afrique: l'influence Bantu à travers le monde swahili et le commerce dans l'Océan Indien. *Bahari* 3:34–40, 1991.

Delaval, Achille. *Les Iles Comores et leur situation politiques.* Nevers: Pointu et Daniel, 1895.

Delhorbe, Clément. Mayotte et les Comores. *Revue de Madagascar* 1:153–174, 1899.

Du Plantier, Nicolas. La Grande Comore; sa colonisation. *Revue Coloniale* 2(3)386–406; 515–548, 1903–1904.

Flobert, Bertrand. *Archipel des Comores: guide d'Anjouan et de Mohéli.* Aix-en-Provence: Makaire, 1973.

Fontoynont, Marurice et E. Raomandahy. La Grande Comore. *Mémoires de l'Académie Malgache* 23, 1937.

Franceschini, E. *Colonies oubliées: Mayotte et les Comores.* Paris, 1886.

Gachet, Christian. *Rapport de mission aux Comores.* Tananarive: Inspection Générale des Eaux et Forêts, 1957.

Gaspart, Claude. Les survivances colonials aux Comoros. In Robin Cohen (ed.), *African Islands and Enclaves.* Beverly Hills: Sage Publications, 1983.

Gérard, Bernard. *Les Comores.* Boulogne-Billancourt: Delroisse, 1974.

Gevrey, A. *Essai sur les Comores.* Pondichery: A. Saligny, 1870.

Gould, D.E. *Let's visit the Comoros.* London: Burke Books, 1985.

Guignard, Alexandre. Rapport sur l'île Mayotte. *Annales maritimes et coloniales* 4:188–198, 1845.

Guillain, M. Mayotte. *Revue de l'Orient* 9:221–236, 1851.

Guilloteaux, Erique. *La Reunion et l'île Maurice, Nossi-Be, et les Comores: leur rôle et leur avenir.* Paris, 1920.

Hanel, Karl. *Madagaskar, Komoren, Reunion.* Bonn: K. Schroeder, 1958.

Heudebert, Lucien. *Au pays des Somalis et des Comoriens.* Paris: Maisonneuve, 1901.

Hocquet, Yves. *La Grande Comore. Pour une meilleure connaissance de l'archipel des Comores.* Paris: CHEAM, 1957.

Hugo, J-F. Communication sur les Comores. *Bulletin des comptes rendus des séances de l'Académie des sciences d'outre-mer* 5, 1974.

Isnard, Hildebert. L'Archipel des Comores. *Les Cahiers d'Outre-mer* 6(21):5–22, 1953.

Janicot, Claude. Les îles comores ouvrent au tourisme leur cadre grandiose. *Connaissance du monde* 40:62–73, 1962.

———. *Madagascar, Comores, Réunion, Ile Maurice.* Paris: Hachette (Les Guides Bleus), 1955.

Lafon, Michel. *Paroles et discours d'Ali Soilihi: Président des Comores 1975–1978.* Paris: CEROI, 1990.

Langenbeck, Rudolf. Die Komoren. *Petermans Mitteilungen* 63:247–249, 1917.

Lavau, G. Les Comores. *Revue de Madagascar* 6:105–132, 1934.

Lionnet, J. F. G. Islands not unto themselves. *Ambio* 12:288–289, 1983.

Lloyd, Tom E. *The forgotten islands.* London: Africa Inland Mission, 1976.

Manicacci, André. Les incursions malgaches aux Comores. *La Revue de Madagascar* 26:73–101, 1939.

Manicacci, Jean. L'Archipel des Comores. *Annales de Géographie* 47:279–290, 1938.

——. *L'Archipel des Comores.* Tananarive: Imprimerie officielle, 1939.

——. L'Archipel des Comores. *L'Encyclopédie Coloniale et Maritime (Madagascar et Réunion).* Paris: Encyclopédie de l'Empire Français, 1947.

——. *Les dependances de Madagascar; l'Archipel des Comores; les terres australes.* Courrier Colonial Illustre Supplement, 1935.

Marquardt, Wilhelm. *Seychellen, Komoren und Maskarenen.* München: Weltforum Verlag, 1976.

——. The small east african islands at the verge of world events. *U.S. Joint Publications Research Service 399:* 4–20 (Translated from Afrika Heute 10:1–9), 1966.

Martin, Jean. L'Archipel des Comores. *Revue française d'études politiques africaines* 44:6–39, 1969.

Moroney, Sean (editor). *Handbooks to the modern world: Africa. Volume I.* New York: Facts on File Publications, 1989.

Newitt, Malyn. *The Comoro Islands: struggle against dependency in the Indian Ocean.* Boulder: Westview Press, 1984.

Ostheimer, John. The politics of comorian independence. Pp. 73–101 in J. Ostheimer (ed.), *The Politics of the Western Indian Ocean.* New York: Praeger, 1975.

——. Political development in the Comoros. *The African Review* 3(3):491–506, 1973.

Ottino, Paul. *Madagascar, les Comoros et le sud-ouest de l'Océan Indien.* Université de Madagascar, 1974.

Richmond, Edmun B. *Language teaching in the Indian Ocean:*

policy and pedagogy in three developing nations (Comoros, Mauritius, and Seychelles). Langham: University Press of America, 1983.

Robequain, C. *Madagascar et les bases dispersées de l'Union Francaise.* Paris: Presses Universitaires de France, 1958.

Roussel, René-A. Visite à N'Tsaouéni, village comorien. *Sciences et Voyages* 75:85–86, 1952.

Said, Ibrahim. Les problèmes de l'Archipel de Comores. *Union Française et parlement* 71:31–32, 1956.

Saint-Alban, Cedric. Les partis politiques comoriens. *Revue Française d'études politiques africaines.* 76–88, 1973.

Saleh, Ibuni. The Comoro Islands. *Tanganyika Notes and Records* 12:51–60, 1941.

Sans, Michel. Anjouan, terre d'Islam. *Encyclopedie Mensuelle d'Outre-Mer* 5(58):270–273, 1955.

———. Archipel des Comores—Comores 53. *Encyclopedie Mensuelle d'Outre-Mer* 4(44):128–131, 1954.

———. L'Archipel des Comores. *Outre-mer* 10:19,27, 1951.

———. Mayotte (Comores). *Encyclopédie mensuelle outre-mer* 30:57–61, 1953.

———. Panorama des Comores. *Études outre-mer* 277–282, 1954.

Saron, G. et R. Lisan. *Madagascar et les Comores.* Paris: Hartmann, n.d.

Southall, Aidan. Research in the western Indian Ocean region conference. *African Studies Bulletin* 9(1):33–37, 1966.

Tara, Vasile et J.-C. Woillet. *Madagascar, Mascareignes et Comores.* Paris: Société Continentale d'Éditions Modernes Illustrées, 1969.

Vérin, Pierre and Rene Battistini. *Les Comores*. Paris: Nathan, 1987.

Willox, Robert. *Madagascar & Comoros*. Hawthorne, Australia: Lonely Planet Publications, 1989.

GEOGRAPHY AND GEOLOGY

Albion, Robert G. *Seaports south of Sahara*. New York: Appleton-Century-Crofts, Inc., 1959.

Aubert de la Rüe, Edgar. Brève note sur l'état actuel du Kartala, volcan de la Grande Comore. *Compte Rendu Sommaire des Séances de la Société Géologique de France* 3/4:54, 1950.

Bachelery, P. et J. Coudray. La Grande Comore et son volcan actif: le Karthala. Aspects géologiques, caractéristiques et évolution de l'activité volcanique. *Le Journal de la Nature* 2(1):32–48, 1990.

Bako Abdou, S. *Brûlante est ma terre*. Paris: L'Harmattan, 1991.

Battistini, René. *L'Afrique Australe et Madagascar*. Paris: P.U.F, 1967.

———. Le volcan actif de la Grande Comore. Madagascar, Revue de Géographie 10/11:41–77, 1967.

Battisini, René and Pierre Vérin. *Géographie des Comores*. Paris: Nathan, 1984.

Boulanger, Jacques. Les tremblements de terre de janvier-février 1953 à la Grande Comore. *Bulletin de l'Académie Malgache* 31:11, 1953.

Bouvet, Henri. Les problèmes de formation aux Comores. *Études Océan Indien* 5, 1985.

Church, R. S. Harrison. The African islands of the Indian Ocean.

Pp. 447–468 in R. S. Harrison Church et al.(eds.), *Africa and the Islands.* New York: Wiley & Sons, 1964.

Cohen, Robin (ed.). *African islands and enclaves.* Sage Series on African Modernization and Development Volume 7. Beverly Hills, CA: Sage Publications, 1983.

Deschamps, Hubert. *Madagascar, Comores, terres australes* (2d ed.). Paris: Berger-Levrault, 1951.

Emerick, C. M. and R. A. Duncan. Age progressive volcanism in the Comores Archipelago, western Indian Ocean and implications for Somali plate tectonics. *Earth and Planetary Sci. Lett.* 60:415–428, 1982.

Esson, J., M.F.J. Flower, D.F. Strong, B.G.J. Upton and W.J. Wadsworth. Geology of the Comores archipelago, western Indian Ocean. *Geological Magazine* 107(6):549–557, 1970.

Gilbert, R. Las Islas Comoras. *Revista geografica americana* 25:44–50, 1946.

Griffin, M. The perfumed isles. *Geography Magazine* 58:524–527, 1986.

Guilcher, A. Coral reefs and lagoons of Mayotte Island, Comoro Archipelago, Indian Ocean, and of New Caledonia, Pacific Ocean. In Whittard, W. F. and R. Bradshaw (eds.), *Submarine Geology and Geophysics.* London: Butterworth Press, 1965.

Guilcher, A., L. Berthois, Y. Le Calvez, R. Battistini, et A. Crosnier. *Les récifs coralliens et le lagon de l'île Mayotte (Archipel des Comores, océan Indien): géomorphologie, sédimentologie, hydrologie, foraminifères.* Paris: ORSTOM, 1965.

Horsey, Algernon de. Great Comoro in 1861. *The Journal of the Royal Geographical Society* 20:258–263, 1864.

———. On the Comoro Islands. *The Journal of the Royal Geographical Society* 34:258–263, 1864.

Humblot, Léon. Les Comores. *Bulletin de la Société de géographie de Paris* 9:386–392, 1886–1887.

Jehenne, Aimable. Renseignements nautique et autres sur l'île Mayotte. *Annales maritimes et coloniales* 2:41–83, 1843.

Lacroix, Alfred. La constitution des roches volcaniques de l'Archipel des Comores. *Comptes Rendus Hebdomadaires des Séances de l'Académie des Sciences* 163:213–219, 1916.

———. La constitution lithologique de l'Archipel des Comores. *Comptes Rendus XIIIe Congrès International Géologique* 2:949–979, 1922, 1925.

———. Une éruption du volcan Karthala, à la Grande Comore, en août 1918. *Comptes Rendus Hebdomadaires des Séances de l'Académie des Sciences* 171:5–10, 1920.

———. *Le volcan actif de l'île de la Réunion (supplément) et celui de la Grande-Comore.* Paris: Gauthier-Villars, 1938.

Marque, I. Le problème de l'eau à la Grande Comore. *Info-Comores.* 46:43–52, 1974.

Maximy, René. *Archipel des Comores: étude géographique.* S.L.N.D., 1973.

———. Moroni, capitale des Comores. Madagascar, *Revue de Géographie* 12:59–80, 1968.

Mondain, J. Note sur une exploration du volcan Karthala (Grand Comore). *Bulletin de l'Académie Malgache* 17:13–24, 1934.

———. Le volcan du Karthala (Grande Comore). *Annales de Physique du Globe de la France d'Outre-Mer* 5:157–158, 1934.

Nougier, J., J. M. Cantagrel, P. Watelet et N. Vatin-Pérignon. Volcanologie de l'île Mayotte (Archipel de Comores). *C. R. Som. Séances Soc. Géol. Fr.* 23(4):139, 1981.

Nougier, J., N. Vatin-Pérignon, J. M. Cantagrel et J. L. Cheminée. Volcanisme et structure de l'île Mayotte (Archipel des Comores). *C. R. Acad. Sc. Paris* 288:211–214, 1979.

Orcel, Paul. Renseignements nautiques sur les îles Comores. *Annales Maritimes et Coloniales* I:652–654, 1844.

Pavlovsky, R. et Jacque de Saint-Ours. *Étude géologique de l'Archipel des Comores.* Tananarive: Service Géologique, 1953.

Pelly, Lewis. Miscellaneous observations upon the Comoro Islands. *Transactions of the Bombay Geographical Society* 16:88–98, 1860–62.

Poirier, Charles. Alluvions asiatique des Comores et de Madagascar. *Mémoire de l'Académie Malgache* 12:59–68, 1848.

Poisson, Charles. Une mission scientifique au volcan Karthala (Grande Comore). *Le Naturaliste Malgache* 1(2):41–51, 1949.

Rasp. Une ascension du volcan Karthala à la Grande Comore. *Annales de Physique du Globe de la France d'Outre-Mer* 4(24)161–169; 171–176, 1937.

Roussel, René-A. Sur le sol tourmenté des Comores, visite au cratère géant du Karthala. *Sciences et Voyages* 22–24, 1953.

Saint-Ours, Jacques de. Étude morphologique et géologique de l'Archipel des Comores. *Bulletin de l'Académie Malgache* 34:7–41, 1956.

———. *Études géologiques dans l'extrême nord de Madagascar et l'Archipel des Comores.* Tananarive: Service Géologique, 1960.

Strong, D. et C. Jacquot. The Karthala caldera, Grande Comore. *Bulletin Volcanologique* 34(3):663–680, 1971.

Strong, D.F. and M.F.J. Flower. The significance of sandstone inclusions in lavas of the Comoros Archipelago. *Earth Planet, Sci. Letters* 7:47–50, 1969.

Tazieff, Haroun. Comores. Pp. 76–86 in *Volcanologues au travail,* tome 2 de *Vingt-cinq ans sur les volcans du globe.* Paris. Fernand Nathan, 1975.

Tomaschek, W. und M. Bittner. *Die topographischen Capitel des indischen Seespiegels Mohit.* Wien: K. K. Geographische Gesselschaft, 1897.

Tricart, J. Reconnaissance geomorphologique de l'Ile d'Anjouan. *Revue de Géographie* 79–107, 1972.

HISTORY AND ARCHAEOLOGY

GENERAL RESEARCH

Aboubaker, Aziza. L'histoire d'Angazija: présentation et traduction des textes arabe, swahili en français. *Études Océan Indien* 1:5–10, 1982.

———. Note sur Bourham Mkelle et l'origine de clans royaux comoriens. *Bulletin des Études Africaines de l'INALCO* 3(5):199–204, 1983.

Allibert, Claude, Alain Argant et Jacqueline Argant. Le site de Bagamoyo (Mayotte, Archipel des Comores). *Études Océan Indien* 2:5–40, 1983.

Allibert, Claude, Alain Argant et Jacqueline Argant. Le site de Dembéni (Mayotte, Archipel des Comores). *Études Océan Indien* 11:63–172, 1990.

Allibert, Claude, Alain Argant et Jacqueline Argant. Brèves notes sur des vestiges trouvés à Mayotte. *Études Océan Indien* 11:179–183, 1990.

Allibert, Claude, Mohamed Ahmed Chamanga, and Georges Boulinier. Texte, traduction et interprétation du Manuscrit de Chingoni (Mayotte). *ASEMI* 7(4):25–62, 1976.

Allibert, Claude et Said Iznouddine. Un document sur les Mafani de Mayotte. *Études Océan Indien* 8:97–109, 1987.

Allibert, Claude. Early Settlement on the Comoro Archipelago. *National Geographic Research* 392–393, 1989.

———. Le manuscrit de Chingoni (Mayotte). *ASEMI* 7(2–3): 119–122, 1976.

———. *Mayotte, plaque tournante et microcosme de l'Océan Indien Occidental, son histoire avant 1841.* Paris: Anthropos, 1984.

———. *Textes anciens sur la côte est de l'Afrique et l'océan Indien occidental.* CEROI, Travaux et documents 8, 1990.

———. Un texte inédit sur l'île d'Anjouan (Comores) (1754) par le britannique R. Orme. INALCO, *Bulletin des Études Africaines* 8(16):125–143, 1988.

———. Une description turque de l'Océan Indien au XVIè siècle: L'Océan Indien Occidental dans le Kitab-i Bahrije de Piri Re'is (1521), Translitération et traduction par Said Khorchid. *Études Océan Indien* 10:9–52, 1988.

Aujas, Louis. Notes historiques et ethnographiques sur les Comores I. *Bulletin de l'Académie Malgache* 9:125–141, 1911.

———. Notes historiques et ethnographiques sur les Comores II. *Bulletin de l'Académie Malgache* 10:183–200, 1912.

Billard, Guy. Note sur la de découverte de traces de civilisations anciennes à Mayotte. ASEMI 8(3–4):256–259, 1977.

Bulpin, T.V. *Islands in a forgotten sea.* Cape Town: Books of Africa, 1969.

Capmartin et Colin. Essai sur les îles Comores. *Annales des voyages de Malte-Brun* 13:144–145, 1810.

Chamisso, Louis de. Une escale aux Comores en 1804. *Historama* 294:122–134, 1976.

Chanudet, Claude. Découverte d'un vieux système fortifié au Namaloungou dans l'intériur de l'île de Mohéli. *Études Océan Indien* 3:191–193, 1983.

———. Site archéologique de Mwali Mdjini à Mohéli. *Études Océan Indien* 12:9–123, 1991.

Chanudet, Claude et Pierre Vérin. Une reconnaisance archéologique de Mohéli. *Études Océan Indien* 2:11–58, 1983.

Cheikh Ioussouf ben el-Moallem Moussa. Histoire de Mayotte et des Sakkalava depuis l'invasion de Radama dans le royaume de Bouéni. *Bulletin de la Société de Géographie de Paris* 20:41–55, 1843.

Chouzour, Sultan. Histoire et Sociologie de Ngazidja: Le manuscrit de Saïd Hussein; Présentation, traduction et notes. *Études Océan Indien* 1:15–54, 1982.

Cidey, G. Chronique arabe de Maoré par Kadhi Owmar Aboubakari (1865). Mayotte: Polycopié, 1980.

Clain, Charles. Emigration africaine dans les colonies de la Reunion, de Nossi-Be, et de Mayotte. *Bulletin de la Société des Études Coloniales et Maritimes* 6:321–325, 1882.

Cornevin, Robert. Les déportés "terroristes" aux Seychelles et aux Comores (1801–1802). *France-Eurafrique* 21(202):15–21, 1969.

Decary, Raymond. Malgaches et Comoriens au temps passé. *Bulletin de Madagascar* 41:18–25, 1951.

Elliot, Reverend. A visit to the island of Johanna. *The United Service Journal* 1:144–152, 1830.

Faurec, Urbain. *L'Archipel aux sultans batailleurs.* Tananarive: Imprimerie officielle, 1941.

——. L'Histoire de l'île de Mayotte. *Cahiers de Madagascar,* 1941.

——. Voyage aux îles Comores. *La Revue de Madagascar* 19:63–107, 1937.

Ferrand, Gabriel. Les îles Ramny, Lamery, Wakwak, Komor des géographes arabes et Madagascar. *Journal Asiatique* 434–566, 1907.

——. *Les Musulmans à Madagascar et aux îles Comores.* 3 Vols. Paris: Ernest Leroux, 1891–1903.

——. Un texte arabico-malgache du XVIe siècle, transcrit, traduit et annoté d'aprés les mss. 7 et 8 de la Bibliothèque Nationale. *Notices et Extraits des Manuscrits de la Bibliothèque Nationale* 38:449–576, 1904.

Freeman-Grenville, G.S.P. and B.G. Martin. A preliminary hand-list of the Arabic inscriptions of the Eastern African coast. *Journal of the Royal Asiatic Society* 2:98–122, 1973.

Froberville, Eugène. Des invasions madécasses aux îles Comores et à la côte orientale d'Afrique. *Annuaire des voyages et de la géographie* 2:194–208, 1845.

Gaba, Djemal-Eddine. Le manuscript arabe de Burhan Mkelle sur la Grande Comore. ASEMI 12(3–4):43–80, 1981.

Grandidier, Guillaume. Les expéditions maritimes des Betsimi-saraka aux Comores. *Revue de l'Afrique orientale et de Madagascar* 20:5–8, 1912.

Grey, Charles. *Pirates of the Eastern Seas 1648–1723*. London, 1933.

Grosset-Grange, H. La cote africaine dans les routiers nautiques arabes au moment des grandes découvertes. *Azania* 13:1–35, 1978.

Guy, Paul. *Mayotte et les comores: essai de chronique judiciaire (1848–1960)*. Paris, 1980.

Guy, Paul et Abdourahamnae ben Chei Amir (trans.). *La vie et l'oeuvre du grand marabout des Comores Said Mohammed ben Al-Ma'arouf (1852–1904)*. Tananarive: Imprimerie Officielle, 1949.

Harries, Lyndon (editor). *The Swahili chronicle of Ngazija* by Said Bakari bin Sultan Ahmed. Bloomington: Indiana University, 1977.

Hebert, Jean-Claude. Documents sur les razzias malgaches aux îles Comores et sur la côte orientale africaine (1790–1820). *Études Océan Indien* 3:5–60, 1983.

Hocquet, Yves. *Contribution à l'histoire politique de l'archipel des Comores*. Paris: CHEAM, 1962.

Jehenne, Aimable. L'île Mayotte. *Revue coloniale*. Annales Maritimes, 1844.

Jones, Sir William. Remarks on the island of Hinzuan, or Johanna. *Asiatic Researches* 2:77–107, 1799.

Jouan, Henri. Les îles Comores. *Bulletin de l'Union géographique du Nord de la France* 253–299, 1883.

———. *Les îles Comores*. Douai: Duthilleuil, 1883.

———. Notes sur les archipels des Comores et des Séchelles. *Mémoires de la Société Impériale des Sciences Naturelles de Cherbourg* 15:45–123, 1869.

Ka'abi, Said. *La vie et l'oeuvre du grand marabout des Comores Said Mohammed ben Ahmed Al-Ma'arouf.* Translated by Paul Guy and Abdourahamane ben Chei Amir. Tananarive, 1949.

Kus, Susan et Henry Wright. Notes préliminaires sur une reconnaissance archéologique de l'île de Mayotte (archipel des Comores). ASEMI 7:123–135, 1976.

Langlois, Louis. *Jomby-Soudy: scènes et récits des îles Comores.* Paris: Joseph Albanel, 1872.

Legras, A. L'île d'Anjouan en 1851. *Bulletin de la Société des sciences et arts de l'île de la Réunion* 162–179 et 258–288, 1866.

Leguevel de Lacombe, B.F. Pages oubliées: un projet d'alliance de la France avec le prince Ramanetake, roi des Comores, et d'établissement à Diégo-Suarez avant 1850. *Revue de Madagascar* 1055–1061, 1906.

Leigh, T.S. Mayotta and the Comoro Islands. *Journal of the Royal Geographical Society* 19:7–17, 1849.

Lignac, Annet. *Les scandales de la Grande Comore.* Paris, 1908.

Lombard-Jourdan, Anne. Une description inédite des îles Comores (1748). *Omaly sy anio, Revue d'Études Historiques,* Université de Tananarive 11:177–203, 1980.

MacCarthy, Oscar. Les îles Comores. Pp. 115–137 in Armand d'Avezac, *Iles de l'Afrique.* Paris: Firmin Didot, 1848.

Manicacci, André. Les incursions malgaches aux Comores. *Revue de Madagascar* 26:73–101, 1939.

Manicacci, Jean. Les derniers terroristes à Anjouan (Comores). *Bulletin de l'Académie Malgache* 29:14–19, 1949.

———. Quatre-vingt-dix annees de colonisation à Mayotte. *Revue de Madagascar* 23:83–109, 1938.

Mantaux, Christian G. Ramanetakarivo et Andriantsolivola dans l'archipel des Comores au XIX siècle. *Bulletin de Madagascar* 22(314–315):554–589, 1948.

Martin, Bradford G. Arab migrations to East Africa in medieval times. *The International Journal of African Historical Studies* 7(3):367–390, 1975.

———. Muslim politics and resistance to colonial rule: Shaykh Uways B. Muhammad Al-Barawi and the qadiriya brotherhood in East Africa. *Journal of African History* 10(3): 471–486, 1969.

———. Notes on some members of the learned classes of Zanzibar and East Africa in the nineteenth century. *African Historical Studies* 4(3):525–545, 1971.

———. A Palestinian Arab and writer on the Comoros. *Études Océan Indien* 6:71–123, 1985.

Martin, Jean. *Comores: quatre îles entre pirates et planteurs.* Paris: L'Harmattan, 1983.

———. Grande Comore 1915 et Anjouan 1940: Etude comparative de dux soulèvements populaires aux Comores. *Études Océan Indien* 3:69–99, 1983.

———. Il y a cent ans la reine de Mohéli rendait visite à Napoléon III. *L'Afrique littéraire et artistique* 4:46–54, 1969.

———. L'affranchissement des esclaves de Mayotte décembre 1846–juillet 1847. *Cahiers d'études africaines* 16:207–233, 1976.

———. Les débuts du protectorat et la révolte servile de 1891 dans l'île d'Anjouan. *Revue française d'histoire d'outre-mer* 60(218):45–85, 1973.

———. Les mémoires de Saïd Hamza el Masela: Une relation de

la vie politique anjouanaise de la fin du XVIIIe siècle à 1840. *Études Océan Indien* 1:109–136, 1982.

———. Un témoignage sur la révolution de 1891 à Anjouan: Le mémoire du prince Salim. *Études Océan Indien* 6:51–70, 1985.

Martin, Jean et H. Chagnoux. The Comoro Islands. *Rev. Fr. Hist.* 69(254):76, 1982.

Martineau, Alfred. Les Comores. Dans Hanotaux, G. et A. Martineau (eds.) *Histoire des Colonies Françaises* 4:281–297, 1934.

Merwart, Paul. *Les colonies françaises, Mayotte et Comores.* Paris: Exposition Universelle, 1900.

Mohamed, Affane. Le premier Coelacanthe capturé dans les eaux comoriennes. *Revue de Madagascar* 37:33–36, 1967.

Mury, Francis. *Aux Comores: les déboires de nos colons. Le rattachement à Madagascar.* Paris: Ch. Lavauzelle, 1908.

Newitt, Malyn. The Comoro Islands in Indian Ocean trade before the nineteenth century. *Proceedings of the International Conference on Indian Ocean Studies.* Perth, 1979.

———. The Karthala caldera, Grande Comore: an historical note. *Bulletin Volcanologique* 38(2):493–494, 1974.

Nicolas du Plantier. La Grand Comore; sa colonisation. *Revue Coloniale* 3:386–406; 515–548, 1903–1904.

Ottenheimer, Martin. A note on the Comoro Islands and East African coastal history. *Folia Orientalia* 18:237–245, 1977.

———. The use of Comorian documents. *History in Africa* 12:349–355, 1985.

Protet, Leopold. L'île Mayotte. *Annales Maritimes et Coloniales* 4:374–377, 1847.

Repiquet, Jules. *Le sultanat d'Anjouan.* Paris: Challamel, 1901.

Ross, Robert. The Dutch on the swahili coast, 1776–1778: two slaving journals, part 1. *International Journal of African Historical Studies* 19(2):305–360, 1986.

Said, Ahmed Zaki. Histoire d'Anjouan. *Promo Al'Camar* 25:36–39; 26:24–31; 27:39–48; 28:39–41, 1971.

Sainsbury, E.B. (ed.). *A calendar of the court minutes, etc. of the East India Company 1644–1649.* Oxford: Clarendon Press, 1912.

Saleh, Ali. El-Maarouf, Grand Marabout des Comores. *Présence Africaine* 224–226, 1974.

———. Le début de l'Islam à la Grande Comore. *Afrika Zamani* 3:23–29, 1974.

———. Une transcription du traité de 1892. *Études Océan Indien* 2:126–134, 1983.

Shepherd, Gillian. M. The Comorians and the East African slave trade. Pp. 73–99 in James L. Watson (ed.), *Asian and African Systems of Slavery.* Oxford: Basil Blackwell, 1980.

Toussaint, Auguste. *Histoire de l'Océan Indien.* Paris: PUF, 1961.

———. *History of the Indian Ocean.* Chicago: University of Chicago Press, 1966.

Valette, Jean. Quelques textes relatifs aux expéditions malgaches aux Comores. *Bulletin de Madagascar* 304:761–764, 1971.

Vérin, Emmanuel Nirina. *Les Comores dans la tourmente: vie politique de l'archipel de la crise de 1976 jusqu'au coup d'etat de 1978.* Paris: CEROI, 1988.

Vérin, Pierre. Contribution à la découverte du patrimoine archéologique aux Comores: observations sur la forteresse ancienne de N'Guni. *Recherche Pédagogie et Culture* 64:50–53, 1983.

———. Guerres civiles comoriennes et invasions malgaches au début du XIXe siècle d'aprés le manuscrit d'Abdoul Latif ben Sultan Msa Foumou. *Bulletin des études africaines de l'Institut national des langues et civilisations orientales* 1:149–160, 1981.

———. Histoire ancienne du nord-ouest de Madagascar. *Taloha* 5. Annales de l'Université de Madagascar, 1972.

———. Les antiquités de l'île d'Anjouan. *Bulletin de l'Académie Malgache* 45(1):69–79, 1968.

———. Les découvreurs placent les Comores sur les cartes du monde. *Études Océan Indien* 10:53–74, 1988.

———. *Les échelles anciennes du commerce sur les côtes nords de Madagascar.* University of Lille, 1975.

———. Mtswa Muyindza et l'introduction de l'Islam à Ngazidja: au sujet de la tradition et du texte de Pechmarty. *Études Océan Indien* 2:95–100, 1983b.

———. Une chronique ancienne sur l'histoire de Mohéli (Mwali). *Études Océan Indien* 12:161–169, 1991.

Vérin, Pierre et Ali Saleh. Une chronique comorienne inconnue: le texte d'Abdel Ghafur Jumbe Fumu. *Études Océan Indien* 1:55–108, 1982.

Vérin, Pierre et Henry Wright. Contribution à l'étude des anciennes fortifications de Ngazidja (Grande Comore). ASEMI 11:289–303, 1981.

Vérin, Pierre et Henry Wright. Les portes de la paix à la Grande-Comore (Fumbuni, Kwambani et Ntsudjini). *Études Océan Indien* 11:173–177, 1990.

Viallard, Paule. Les antiquitiés de la Grande Comore. *Taloha* 4:169–184, 1971.

Vienne, Emile. *Notice sur Mayotte et les Comores.* Paris: Exposition Universelle, 1900.

Voeltzkow, Alfred. Bericht über eine Reise nach Ost-Afrika zur Untersuchung der Bildung...(IV. Die comoren). *Zeitschrift der Gesellschaft für Erdkunde zu Berlin* 39:279–301, 1904.

———. Die Comoren. *Zeitschrift der Gesellschaft für Erdkunde zu Berlin* 41:606–630, 1906.

Wright, Henry. Early communities on the island of Maore and the coasts of Madagascar. Pp. 53–88 in C. Kottak et al. (eds.) *Madagascar: Society and History.* Durham: Carolina Academic Press, 1979.

Wright, Henry. Early seafarers of the Comoro Islands: the dembeni phase of the IX-X centuries A.D. *Azania* 19:13–60, 1984.

Zaki, Saïd Ahmed. Histoire d'Anjouan. *Promo Al'Camar* 25–28, 1971.

Zaouali, Mohamed. Un texte arabe relatif à la Grande Comore recueilli à Madagascar par Gabriel Ferrand. ASEMI 12(3–4):81–93, 1981.

VOYAGERS' NARRATIVES

Allibert, Claude et Florence Vérin. *Deux voyages inédits sur Madagascar et les Comores autour de 1840: J. S. Leigh et J. Marshall.* Paris: CEROI, Travaux et Documents 15, 1991.

Bajot, M. Extrait de la relation d'un voyage fait à Madagascar, à Anjouan et aux Seychelles pendant les années 1818–1819 par M. Frappas, Enseigne de vaisseau. *Annales Maritimes et*

Coloniales 1re serie, 2e partie:229 and 258–259. Paris, 1820.

Barnard, Lieut. R.N. *A three years cruise in the Mozambique Channel.* London: Dawsons of Pall Mall, 1969.

Beehler, W.H. *The cruise of the Brooklyn.* Philadelphia: J.B. Lippincott & Co., 1885.

Boteler, Thomas. *Narrative of a voyage of discovery to Africa and Arabia.* London, 1835.

Bourde, André. Un comorien aventureux au XIXe siècle: l'extra-ordinaire voyage du prince Aboudou. Pp. 265–290 in *Sixième colloque international d'histoire maritime, Méditerranée et Océan Indien* (Venise, 1962). Paris: SEVPEN, 1970.

Brissot-Thivars, L.S. (editor). *Memoires du Capitaine Peron sur Se Voyages aux Côte d'Afrique, en Arabie, aux îles d'Amesterdam, aux îles d'Anjouan et de Mayotte.* Paris: Brissot-Thivars, 1824.

Burnell, A.C. and Tiele, P.A. (eds.). *The voyage of John Huyghen van-Linschoten to the East Indies* (2 vols.) London: The Hakluyt Society, 1884.

Colomb, Philip Howard. *Slave catching in the Indian Ocean, a record of naval experiences.* Atlantic Highlands, NJ: Humanities Press, 1968 (originally published 1873).

Decary, Raymond. Un voyage aux Comores il y a un siècle et demi. *Revue de Madagascar* 31:47–56, 1957.

Decken, Baron Carl Clause von der. *Reisen in Ost-afrika in dem Jahren 1859 bis 1865.* 2 volumes. Leipzig: C. F. Winter, 1871.

Ferrand, G. *Rélations des voyages et textes geographiques*

Arabes, Persans et Turqs relatif a l'Extreme-Orient du VIIIe au XVIIIe siècles. Paris: Librairie Leroux, 1913.

Foster, Sir William (editor). *The embassy of Sir Thomas Roe*. London: The Hakluyt Society, 1899.

Foster, Sir William (editor). *The voyages of Sir James Lancaster*. London: The Hakluyt Society, 1940.

Gray, A. (editor). *The voyage of Francis Pyrard*. London: The Hakluyt Society, 1887–1890.

Grose, John Henry. *A voyage to the East Indies, with observations on various ports there*. London: S. Hooper and A. Morley, 1757.

Hair, P.E.H. Material on Africa (other than the Mediterranean and Red Sea lands) and on the Atlantic islands, in the publications of Samuel Purchas, 1613–1626. *History in Africa* 13:117–159, 1986.

Horsburgh, James. *India Directory: a direction for sailing to and from the East Indies*. London, 1817.

Langhans, Paul. Dr. K.W. Schmidts Reisen auf den westlichen Komoren. *Petermans Mitteilungen* 36:11–15, 1890.

Le Bron de Vexela. Voyage à Madagascar et aux îles Comores (Quatrième article). *Revue de l'Orient* 10:51–66, 1846.

Leguevel de Lacombe, B.F. *Voyage à Madagascar et aux îles Comores*. Paris: Louis Delessart, 1840.

Lelieur de Ville-sur-arce, William. Relation de la campagne de la goélette de S. M. le Lys, . . . description des îles Comores, Anjouan, Mohéli et Mayotte. . . . *Annales maritimes et coloniales,* 1821.

Markham, Albert Hastings (ed.). *The voyages and works of John Davis, the navigator*. New York: Burt Franklin, n.d. Reprint of 1880 edition.

Molet, Louis et Anne Sauvaget. Les voyages de Peter Mundy au XVIIe siècle (2e partie: les Comores). *Bulletin de Madagascar* 298:3–27, 1971.

Moussa Said. Le périple d'un Comorien de Zanzibar à Mascate et retour. *Études Océan Indien* 10:103–122, 1988.

Mundy, Peter. *The travels of Peter Mundy 1608–1667.* London: Hakylut Society, 1919.

Ovington, John. Description of Madagascar and the island Anjouan. *A Voyage to Suratt in 1689.* London: J. Tonson, 1690.

Owen, W.F.W. *Narrative of voyages to explore the shores of Africa, Arabia, and Madagascar.* London: Richard Bentley, 1833 (Republished 1968 by Gregg International Publishers Limited).

Payton, Walter. A journal of all principal matters passed in the twelfth voyage to the East-India. *Hakluytus Posthumus or Purchas his Pilgrimes* (Vol. 4). Samuel Purchas ed. Glasgow: James Maclehose and Sons, 1905.

Prior, James. *Voyage along the eastern coast of Africa to Mozambique, Johanna and Quiloa in the Nisus Frigate.* London: Phillips, 1819.

Rotter, Gernot. *Die Komoren-Chronik des Qadi 'Ilmarb. Ab. Bakr.* Tuebingen, 1973.

———. (trans. & ed.). *Muslimische inseln vor Ost Afrika:* eine arabische Komoren-Chronile des 19 Jahrhunderts by 'Umar ibn Ab. Bakr Sirazi. Beirut: Steiner, 1976.

Schmidt, Karl-Wilhelm. Reisen auf den westlichen Komoren. *Petermann's Mitteilungen* 11–15, 1886.

Strachan, Michael and Boies Penrose (editors). *The East India Company journals of Captain William Keeling and Master Thomas Bonner, 1615–1617.* Minneapolis: University of Minnesota Press, 1971.

Voeltzkow, Alfred. *Reise in Ostafrika in den Jahren 1903–1905.* Stuttgart: E. Schweizerbart'sche, 1914.

LANGUAGE

Aboubaker, Aziza. Le manuscrit de Burhan Mkelle et la langue comorienne. *Études Océan Indien* 2:117–122, 1983.

Ahmed-Chamanga, Mohamed. L'accentuation du verbal en shindzuani (Anjouanais, îles Comores). *Afrique et Langage* 25:35–54, 1986.

———. Propositions pour une écriture standard du comorien. ASEMI 7(2–3):73–80, 1976.

Ahmed-Chamanga, Mohamed et Noël Jacques Gueunier. *Le dictionnaire Comorien-français et Français-comorien du R. P. Sacleux.* Paris: SELAF, 1979.

Ahmed-Chamanga, Mohamed et Noël Jacques Gueunier. Récherches sur l'instrumentalisation du comorien: problèmes d'adaptation lexicale d'après la version comorienne de la loi du 23 novembre 1974. *Cahiers d'Études Africanes* 17(66–67): 213–239, 1977.

Ahmed-Chamanga, Mohamed et Noël Jacques Gueunier. Récherches sur l'instrumentalisation du comorien: les problèmes de graphie d'après la version comorienne de la loi du 23 novembre 1974. ASEMI 8(3–4):45–77, 1977.

Ahmed-Chamanga, Mohamed, M. Lafon et J.-L. Sibertin-Blanc. Projet d'orthographe pratique du comorien. *Etudes Océan Indien* 9:7–33, 1988.

Angot, M. Grammaire anjouanaise. *Bulletin de l'Académie Malgache* 27:89–123, 1946.

Aujas, Louis. Rémarques sur quelques étymologies de noms de lieux géographiques à Mayotte. *Revue d'Ethnographie et des Tradition Populaires* 1:51–59, 1920.

Benson, C. W. Noms comoriens d'oiseaux. *Le Naturaliste malgache* 13:265–268, 1962.

Blanchy, Sophie. *L'interprete: lexique mahorais-francais et français-mahorais.* Mayotte: C.M.A.C. et Editions Kashkasi, 1987.

Boulinier, Georges. Linguistique comorienne: note bibliographique. *Journal des Africanistes* 46(1–2):223–226, 1976.

Cassimjee, Farida and Charles W. Kisseberth. Shingazidja nominal accent. *Studies in the Linguistic Sciences* 19(1):33–61, 1989.

Cheikh Moinaesha. *Morphologie du verbe dans la langue comorienne (G-C.).* Aix-en-Provence: Maîtrise de lettres modernes, 1981.

Damir ben Ali. Commentaires sur quelques termes de la version arabe du Habara na Angazidja. *Études Océan Indien* 1:11–14, 1982.

Elliot, W. A grammar and vocabulary of the Hinzuan language. In M. Heepe, Darstellung einer Bantusprache aus den Jahren 1821–22. *Mitteilungen des Seminars für Orientalische Sprachen an der Friedrich-Wilhelms Universität zu Berlin* 29(3):199–232, 1926.

Fischer, F. *Grammaire-dictionaire comorien.* Strasbourg: Société d'Editions de la Basse-Alsace, 1949.

Gueunier, Noël J. Lexique du dialecte malgache de Mayotte (Comores). *Études Océan Indien* 7, 1986.

———. Notes sur le dialecte malgache de l'île de Mayotte (Comores). *Asie du sud-est et monde insulindien* 7(2–3):81–118, 1976.

———. Un système d'écriture arabico-malgache à Mayotte (Comores). ASEMI 12(3–4):95–107, 1981.

Hair, P. E. H. The earliest extant word-list of swahili, 1613. *African Studies* 40(2):151–153, 1981.

Harris, Zellig. The phonemes of swahili based on the speech of a native of Grande-Comore. Pp. 97–124 in Z. Harris, *Structural Linguistics*. Chicago: University of Chicago Press, 1951.

Heepe, M. Darstellung einer bantusprache aus den jahren 1821/22 von Elliot. *Mitteilungen des Seminars für Orientalische Sprachen* 3:191–232, 1926.

——. Die Komorendialekte Ngazidja, Nzwani, und Mwali. *Abhanlungen des Hamburgischen Kolonialinstituts* 23:1–166, 1920.

Hildebrandt, J. M. Fragmente der johanna-sprache. *Zeitschrift für Ethnologie* 8:89–96, 1876.

Johnston, Sir Harry. *A comparative study of the Bantu and Semi-Bantu languages*. Oxford: Clarendon Press, 1922.

Jouannet, Francis. *Des tons à l'accent, essai sur l'accentuation du comorien*. Univ. de Provence Aix-Marseille 1, 1989.

Lafon, Michel. A propos d'un dictionnaire shingazidja-français. In J. Hutchinson and V. Manfredit (eds.) *Current Issues in African Linguistics* 7:73–87. Dordrecht: Foris, 1990.

——. Brève présentation du système verbal et du fonctionnement d'un auxiliare en shingazidja. *Oralitè Documents* 4:151–177, 1982.

——. *Le shingazidja, une langue bantu sous influence arabe*. Paris: INALCO, 1987.

——. Lexique français-shingazidja. *Travaux et documents du CEROI* 14. Paris: INALCO, 1991.

——. Négation de la prédication en shingazidja. *Linguistique africaine* 4:123–144, 1990.

——. Petit vocabulaire français-shingazidja à l'usage des amateurs. *Travaux et documents du CEROI* 7. Paris: INALCO, 1989.

——. Régularité et irrégularité dans le système verbal du shingazidja (grand-comorien). *Afrique et Langage* 22:5–34, 1984.

——. Situation linguistique à la Grande-Comore, essai de définition du statut de l'arabe. *Matériaux arabes et sud-arabiques* 95–119, 1988–89.

——. Un procédé d'emphase en shingazidja, étude descriptive. *Bulletin des Études Africaines de l'INALCO* 9:3– 36, 1985.

Lafon, Michel and Jean-Luc Sibertin-Blanc. *Langues et contacts de langues dans l'archipel des Comores.* Paris: INALCO, 1975.

Möhlig, Wilhelm, G. Philippson, M.-F. Rombi, et J. C. Winter. Classification dialectométrique de quelques parlers swahilis (swahili du nord et swahili comorien). Pp. 267–304 dans Guarisma, Gladys et S. Platiel (eds.), *Dialectologie et Comparatisme en Afrique Noire.* Paris: SELAF, 1980.

Nurse, Derek. Is Comorian Swahili? Being an examination of the diachronic relationship between Comorian and coastal Swahili. Pp. 83–105 in M-F Rombi (ed.), *Le swahili et ces limites.* Paris: Editions sur les civilisations, 1989.

Ormières, R. *Lexique français-anjouanais.* Paris: Imprimerie Polyglotte Hugonis, 1893.

Ottenheimer, Harriet. *ShiNzwani-English Dictionary with English-ShiNzwani Finderlist.* Manhattan, KS: Comorian Studies-SASW, 1986.

Ottenheimer, Harriet and Martin Ottenheimer. The classification of the languages of the Comoro Islands. *Anthropological Linguistics* December:408–415, 1977.

Ottenheimer, Harriet and Heather Primrose. Current research on ShiNzwani ideophones. *Studies in the Linguistic Sciences* 19(2):77–87, 1989.

Philippson, Gérard. L'accentuation du comorien, essai d'analyse métrique. *Études Océan Indien* 9:35–79, 1988.

———. Observations sur une étude récente de morphologie verbale de la langue comorienne. *Études Océan Indien* 2:123–126, 1983.

Rey, Véronique. Détermination des schèmes accentuels du système verbal en shingazidja. *Travaux de l'Institut de Phonétique d'Aix* 12:129–152, 1988.

Rombi, Marie-Françoise (ed.). *Études sur le bantu oriental, langues des Comores, de Tanzanie, de Somalie et du Kénya.* Paris: SELAF, 1982.

Rombi, Marie-Françoise. La nasalité en ngazija (Grande Comore). *Revue d'Éthnolinguistique* 4:59–81, 1989.

———. *Le shimaore (île de Mayotte, Comores): première approche d'un parler de la langue comorienne.* Paris: SELAF, 1983.

Rombi, Marie-Françoise et Pierre Alexandre. Les parlers comoriens: caractéristiques différentielles; position par rapport au swahili. Pp. 17–39 in M.-F. Rombi (ed.), *Études sur le bantu oriental, langues des Comores, de Tanzanie, de Somalie et du Kénya.* Paris: SELAF, 1982.

Saleh, Ali. *Cours d'initiation a la langue comorienne.* Paris: G.-P. Maisonneuve et Larose, 1979.

———. Le swahili, langue véhiculaire de l'Afrique Orientale et des Comores. *Revue Française d'Études Politiques Africaines* 70:82–94, 1971.

Sibertin-Blanc, J.-L. Sur quelques aspects des dialectes comoriens en contraste avec le kiswahili. *EACROTANAL studies and documents* 1:33–68, 1980.

Steere, E. *Short specimens of the vocabularies of three unpublished African languages.* London, 1869.

Struck, B. An unpublished vocabulary of the Comoro language. *African Society Journal* 8:412–421, 1909.

Tucker, A.N. and M.A. Bryan. Tonal classification of nouns in Ngazija. *African Language Studies* 11:351–383, 1970.

PLANTS AND ANIMALS

Abdallah, Mirghane. *La pêche maritime aux îles Comores.* Bruxelles-Moroni: Association pour la promotion de l'Education et de la Formation à l'Étranger, 1985.

Adjanohoun, E.J., L. Aké Assi, Ali Ahmed, J. Eymé, S. Guinko, A. Kayonga, A. Keita, et M. Lebras. *Contribution aux études ethnobotaniques et floristiques aux Comores.* Paris: ACCT, 1982.

Benson, C.W. Birds of the Comoro Islands. *Ibis* 103:55–106, 1960.

Clymer, Eleanor. *Search for a living fossil.* New York: Scholastic Book Services, 1970.

Cornevin, Robert. La botanique au secours de l'histoire. *France-Eurafrique* 21(205):43–44, 1969.

Fischer-Piette, E. et D. Vukadinovic. Les mollusques terrestres des îles comores. *Mémoires du Muséum National d'Histoire Naturelle de Paris* 84:1–76, 1974.

Fourmanoir, P. *Ichtyologie et Peche aux Comores.* Memoire de l'Institut Scientifique de Madagascar, n.d.

Fricke, H. and R. Plante. Habitat requirements of the living coelacanth *Latimeria chalumnae* at Grande Comore, Indian Ocean. Naturwissenschaft 75:149–151, 1988.

Gachet, Christian. *Étude des problèmes forestiers de l'archipel des Comores.* Tananarive: Centre forestier tropical, 1964.

———. Tourisme forestier aux îles Comores. *Revue de Madagascar* 4:40–59, 1958.

Grottanelle, V.L. *Pescatori dell'Oceano Indiano.* Rome, 1955.

Jodot, J. Peuplement de Madagascar et des Archipels voisins par les mollusques continentaux, leur liaison avec la classification du Quaternaire. *Mémoires de l'Institut de Madagascar* 4(2):131–167, 1952.

Newton, Edward. On a collection of birds from the Island of Anjuan. *Proceedings of the Zoological Society of London* 295–302, 1877.

Prosperi, Franco. *Au royaume des coraux: De Zanzibar à la Grande Comore.* Paris: Julliard, 1956.

———. *Vanished Continent; an Italian expedition to the Comoro Islands.* London: Hutchinson, 1957.

Smith, J.L.B. *Old Fourlegs; the Story of the Coelacanth.* London: Longman, Green, 1956.

Tattersall, Ian. Ecology and Behavior of Lemur Fulvus Mayottensis (Primates, Lemuri formes). *Anthropological Papers of the American Museum of Natural History* 54:421–482, 1977.

———. Group Structure and Activity Rhythm in *Lemur mongoz* on Anjouan and Moheli Islands, Comoro Archipelago. *Anthropological Papers of the American Museum of Natural History* 53:367–380, 1976.

———. The Lemurs of the Comoro Islands. *Oryx* 13:445–448, 1977.

———. Patterns of Activity in the Mayotte lemur, Lemur fulvus mayottensis. *J.Mammal* 60:314–323, 1979.

———. Studies on the Lemurs of the Comoro Archipelago. *National Geographic Society Research Reports* 15:641–654, 1983.

Tattersall, Ian and R.W. Sussman. Island Primates of the Western Indian Ocean. *Research Reports, National Geographic Society* 856–862, 1976.

Thomson, Keith S. The capture and study of two coelacanths off the Comoro Islands, 1972. *National Geographic Society Research Reports* 13: 615–622, 1981.

———. *Living fossil: the story of the coelacanth.* New York: W. W. Norton & Company, 1991.

———. The second coelacanth. *American Scientist* 77:536–538, 1989.

———. Secrets of the coelacanth. *Natural History* 82(2):58–65, 1973.

CULTURE AND SOCIETY

Abdoulkarim, M. et A. Taburet. *Étude succincte des caractéristiques économiques et sociales du milieu rural comorien - place et rôle de la femme dans ce milieu.* Rapport d'enquête PNUD/FAO/UNICEF. Ministère de la production et du développement industriel, Comores, 1980.

Ahmed-Chamanga, Mohamed. Chansons comoriennes modernes. *Ambario* 1(2–3):189–199, 1978.

————. Pucelle cochon: conte anjouanais. *Études Océan Indien* 8:129–141, 1987.

————. *Rois, femmes et djinns: contes de l'île d'Anjouan.* Paris: CEROI, 1988.

Al-Ma-arouf, Said Mohammed Ben Ahmed. *La vie et l'oeuvre; du grand Marabout des Comores.* Tananarive, 1949.

Ali, Mohamed Djalim. Esquisse d'une étude sur le peuplement des Comores: entre Bantu et Arabes. *Bahari* 3:29–33, 1991.

Allibert, Claude. *Contes mahorais.* Paris: Centre Universitaire Méditerranéen et Académie des Sciences d'Outre-Mer, 1980.

Bencheikh, Touhami. Régulation familiale aux Comores: une déclaration du grand Mufti Mohammed Abderrahame. *Études Océan Indien* 6:35–40, 1985.

Blanchy, Sophie. Culture et personnalité aux Comores: rélations familiales et sociales, le style des interactions, l'espoir trans-culturel. *Actes du Colloque de Psychiatrie* 3:121–131. Université de la Réunion: Paris, 1990.

————. Eléments pour une étude anthropologique des pratiques thérapeutiques à Mayotte (Comores). *Revue l'Espoir Transculturel* 2:32–41, 1989.

————. Le monde invisible dans le vie traditionelle aux Comores. *Revue L'Espoir Transculturel* 2:6–20, 1989.

————. Le tambour, conte comorien de Mayotte. *Revue l'Espoir Transculturel* 2:20–32, 1989.

————. *Lignée féminine et valeurs islamiques à travers quelques contes de Mayotte, archipel des Comores.* Mémoire pour le D.E.A. d'Anthropologie. Université de La Réunion, 1986.

————. Mères et filles dans les contes de Mayotte. Pp. 131–169 in

L'enfant dans les contes in Afrique, sous la direction de V. Gorog-Karady. Paris: Ed. CILF/EDICEF, Coll. Textes et civilisations, 1988.

———. Parole et proverbes à Mayotte. *Cahiers de Littérature Orale* 20:161–178. Paris, 1985.

———. Proverbes mahorais. ASEMI 12(3–4):109–132, 1981.

Blanchy, Sophie et Saïd Moussa. Inscriptions religieuses et magico-religieuses sur les monuments historiques à Ngazidja (Grande-Comore): le sceau de Salomon. *Études Océan Indien* 11:7–62, 1990.

Blanchy, Sophie et Zaharia Soilihi. *Furukombe et autres contes de Mayotte, textes bilingues.* Paris: Éditions Caribéennes-CMAC de Mayotte, 1991.

Blanchy-Daurel, Sophie. *La vie quotidienne a Mayotte (Archipel des Comores).* Paris: L'Harmattan, 1990.

Boulinier, Georges. Les princesses shirazi de la Grande Comore ou un autre visage des Mille et Une Nuits. *Cahiers de littérature orale* 17:129–162, 1985.

———. Traditions relatives a l'introduction de l'Islam a la Grande Comore. ASEMI 12(3–4):15–42, 1981.

Boulinier, Georges and Geneviève Boulinier-Giraud. Chronologie de la pirogue à balancier: le témoignage de l'Océan Indian occidental. *Journal de la Société des Océanistes* 23(50):89–98, 1976.

Boulinier, Georges and Geneviève Boulinier-Giraud. Mission 1973 aux Comores (Anthropologie biologique et ethnologie). ASEMI 5(1):207–222, 1973.

Boulinier, Georges et Geneviève Boulinier-Giraud. Volcanisme et traditions populaires à la Grande Comore. ASEMI 7(2–3):45–71, 1976.

Breslar, John, Bernard Chatain et Léon Attila Cheyssial. *Habitat mahorais, étude analytique et perspectives.* Paris: AG.G., 1979.

Brye, Emmanuel de. L'enfant comorien et l'apprentissage de l'Islam: Quelques observations. *Études Océan Indien* 6:41–50, 1985.

Chaher. La Polygamie. *Activités:* 4eme trimèstre, 1965.

Chouzour, Sultan. *Idéologie et institutions: l'Islam aux Comores.* Mémoire de maîtrise de Philosophie. Aix-en-Provence: Faculté des Lettres et Sciences Humaines, 1972.

———. Propos de Saïd Husein et compréhension de la civilisation comorienne. *Études Océan Indien* 2:101–116, 1983.

———. Un témoignage d'une littérature nationale méconnue: l'oeuvre du Prince Saïd Husein; extraits relatifs aux proverbes et aux contes des bouffons. *Bulletin des Études Africaines de l'INALCO* 3(5):43–64, 1983.

Damir ben Ali. Musiques traditionnelle et religieuse des Comores. *Ya Mkobe* 1:49–52, 1983.

———. Organisation sociale et politique des Comores avant le XVe siècle. *Ya Nkobe* 1:25–34, 1984.

Damir ben Ali, George Boulinier et Paul Ottino. *Traditions d'une lignée royale des Comores.* Paris: L'Harmattan, 1985.

Damir ben Ali and Mohamed Elhad. Place et prestige du swahili dans les îles Comores. *Ya Nkobe* 1:12–16, 1984.

Decary, Raymond. Poupées malgaches et comoriennes. *Revue de Madagascar* 20:41–52, 1937.

Delisle, F. Sur un crane de la Grand-Comore. *Bulletin et Memoires. Société d'Anthropologie de Paris,* 5th Series 8:450–457. Paris, 1907.

Delval, Raymond. Le monde arabe vu des îles de l'Océan Indien occidental. *Sociétés africaines, monde arabe et culture islamique.* Mémoires du CEERMA 2, 1981.

———. L'Islam aux Comores. *Mondes et Cultures* 40(1):127–140, 1980.

Dussert, P. L'agriculture à Mayotte et aux Comores. *L'Agriculture Pratique des Pays Chauds* 96:206–214, 1911.

Flobert, Bertrand. *Les Comores, évolution juridique et sociopolitique.* Aix-Marseille: CEROI, 1976.

Flobert, Thierry. *Les Comores: evolution juridique et socio-politique.* Aix-en-Provence: Centre d'Études et de Récherches sur les sociétés de l'Océan Indien, 1976.

Galabru, Jean-Jacques. *La Grande Comore, terre d'Islam et de coutumes.* Mémoire d'entrée. Centre des Hautes Études sur l'Afrique et l'Asie Modernes, 1952.

Gueunier, Noël J. *La belle ne se marie point: contes comoriens en dialecte malgache de l'île de Mayotte.* Paris: Peeters-SELAF, 1990.

———. Le Chat et le Rat, conte en dialecte malgache de l'île de Mayotte (Comores). *Afrique et Langage* 4:30–45, 1975.

Gueunier, Noël J. et Jean Luc Sibertin. Le monstre dévorant: un conte malgache en dialecte sakalava et une conte comorien en dialecte shimaore. *Études Océan Indien* 8:21–56, 1987.

Guy, Paul. Islam Comorien in J. Berque (ed.) *Normes et valeurs dans l'Islam contemporain.* Paris, 1966.

———. Le mariage en droit comorien. *Rev. jurid, et pol. U.F.* 2:307–346, 1955.

132 / Selected Bibliography

———. Le mariage en droit comorien. *Rev. jurid, et pol. U.F.* 4:799–830, 1956.

———. Le Minhadj-et-Twalibin et les coutumes comoriennes dans le statut personnel. *Études Océan Indien* 6:7–34, 1985.

———. *L'Islam aux Comores.* Paris: CHEAM, 1956.

———. Sur une coutume locale de droit musulman de l'Archipel de Comores. *Revue Algérienne Tunisieenne et Marocaine de législation et de jurisprudence.* Octobre - Décembre: 73–79, 1942.

———. *Traité de droit musulman comorien.* Alger, 1954.

———. *Traité de droit musulman comorien, tome 1, Le statut personnel: le mariage.* Paris: CHEAM, 1956.

———. Une adaptation doctrinale à une carence momentanée de la jurisprudence comorienne. *Études Océan Indien* 2:135–141, 1983.

Hebert, Jean-Claude. Analyse structurale des géomancies comoriennes, malgaches et africaines. *Journal de la Société des Africanistes* 21(2):115–203, 1961.

———. Fêtes agraires dans l'île d'Anjouan. *Journal de la Société des Africanistes.* 30(1):101–116, 1960.

———. Le calendrier et la fête du Nairûz en Afrique Orientale, aux Comores et à Madagascar. *Langues, cultures et sociétés de l'Océan Indien,* 1981.

Hornell, J. The outrigger canoes of Madagascar, East Africa, and the Comoro Islands. *The Mariner's Mirror* 30(1):3–18; 30(4):170–185, 1944.

Inzouddine, Said et Michel Lafon. On a marché sur la lune. *Études Océan Indien* 10:131–138, 1988.

Lambek, Michael. Certain knowledge, contestable authority: power and practice on the Islamic periphery. *American Ethnologist* 17(1):23–40, 1990.

———. Exchange, time, and person in Mayotte: the structure and destructuring of a cultural system. *American Anthro-pologist* 92(3):647–661, 1990.

———. Graceful exits: spirit possession as personal performance in Mayotte. *Culture* 8:59–69, 1988.

———. *Human spirits: a cultural account of trance in Mayotte.* New York: Cambridge University Press, 1981.

———. Like teeth biting tongue: the proscription and practice of spouse abuse in Mayotte. Pp. 157–171 in Dorothy Ayers Counts, Judith K. Brown, and Jacquelyn C. Campbell (eds.), *Sanctions and sanctuary: cultural perspectives on the beating of wives.* Boulder: Westview Press, 1992.

———. Motherhood and other careers in Mayotte. Pp. 76–92 in J. K. Brown and V. Kerns (eds.), *In her prime: new views of middle-aged women.* 2nd Edition. Urbana: University of Illinois Press, 1992 (Originally published in 1985 by Bergin and Garvey).

———. The playful side of Islam and its possible fate in Mayotte. *Communication au Colloque International d'His-toire Malgache.* Antsiranana, 1987.

———. The practice of Islamic experts in a village on Mayotte. *Journal of Religion in Africa* 20(1):20–40, 1990.

———. Spirit and spouses: possession as a system of communication among the Malagasy speakers of Mayotte. *American Ethnologist* 7(2):318–331, 1980.

———. Spirit possession/spirit succession: aspects of social continuity in Mayotte. *American Ethnologist* 15:710–731, 1988.

———. Virgin marriage and the autonomy of women in Mayotte. *Signs: Journal of Women in Culture and Society* 9(2):264–281, 1983.

Lambek, Michael (with J. Lambek). The kinship terminology of Malagasy speakers in Mayotte. *Anthropological Linguistics* 23(4):154–82, 1981.

Lambek, Michael and Jon H. Breslar.. Funerals and social change in Mayotte. Pp. 393–410 in Conrad Phillip Kottak, Jean-Aimé Rakotoarisoa, Aidan Southall, and Pierre Vérin (eds.), *Madagascar: Society and History.* Durham, NC: Carolina Academic Press, 1986.

Le Fur, Yves, Jean-Claude Pichard, and Anne-Marie Pichard-Libert. *Bangas, Mayotte.* Mayotte: Editions Bo'wi, 1989.

Le Guennec-Coppens, Françoise. Le manyahuli grand-comorien: un système de transmission des biens peu orthodoxe en pays musulman. Pp. 257–268 in Marceau Gast (ed.), *Hériter en pays musulman.* Paris: CNRS, 1987.

Mantoux, T. Notes socio-économiques sur l'archipel des Comores. *Revue française d'études politiques africaines* 100, 1974.

Maroger, C. and C. Lecointre. Le recensement général de la population de Mayotte de 1978. Pp. 249–296 in *Recensements africains.* Paris: Groupe de Travail de Démographie Africaine, 1981.

Martin, Jean. Les notions de clans, nobles et notables: leur impact dans la vie politique Comorienne d'aujourd'hui. *L'Afrique et l'Asie* 81/82:39–63, 1968.

Mas, J. La loi des femmes et la loi de Dieu (à propos d'une coutume grand-comorienne). *Annuaire des Pays de l'Océan Indien* 6:103–126, 1979.

Massignon, Louis. Les sept dormants d'Ephèse (Ahl al-Kahf) en

Islam et en Chrétienté, 8e partie: note sur les VII dormants aux îles Comores. *Revue des Études Islamiques* 30(1):1–5, 1962.

Mkufundi, Mariama Ali. L'origine des gens aux Comores et la coutume du Manyahuli (translated by Aziza Aboubakar). *Études Océan Indien* 1:149–151, 1982.

Ottenheimer, Harriet J. Culture contact and musical style: ethnomusicology in the Comoro Islands. *Ethnomusicology* 14(3):458–462, 1970.

Ottenheimer, Harriet and Martin Ottenheimer. The collection from the Comoro Islands. *Resound, Quarterly of the Archives of Traditional Music at Indiana University* 1:1–2, 1982.

Ottenheimer, Martin. *Marriage in Domoni.* Prospect Heights, IL: Waveland Press, 1985.

———. Multiethnicity and trade in the western Indian Ocean area. In W. Arens (ed.), *A Century of Change in Eastern Africa.* The World Anthropology Series. Sol Tax (series ed.), The Hague: Mouton, 1976.

Ottenheimer, Martin and Harriet Ottenheimer. Matrilocal residence and nonsororal polygyny. *Journal of Anthropological Research* 35(3):328–335, 1979.

Ottenheimer, Martin and Harriet Ottenheimer. Music of the Comoro Islands—Domoni. *Folkways Records* FE4243, 1982; Smithsonian/Folkways Records 04243, 1992.

Raynal, J. Enquête sanitaire à la Grande Comore en 1925. Observation de paludisme à forme endémique. *Bulletin de la Société de Pathologie Exotique* 21:35–54; 132–141.

Robert, Michel. *La société islamique et le droit musulman aux Comores et dans l'Océan Indien.* D.E.S. histoire de Institutions. Univ. Paris II, 1976.

Robineau, Claude. *Approche sociologique des Comores (Ocean Indian).* Paris: ORSTOM, 1962.

——. Approche socio-économique d'Anjouan. *Cahiers de l'Institute de Science Economique Appliquée* 139:63–106, 1963.

——. L'islam aux Comores. *Taloha* 2:39–55, 1966.

——. L'islam aux Comores: une étude d'histoire culturelle de l'île d'Anjouan. *Revue de Madagascar* 35:17–34, 1966.

——. Société et économie d'Anjouan (Océan Indien). *Mémoires ORSTOM* 21, 1966.

Rombi, Marie-Françoise et Mohamed Ahmed Chamanga. *Contes Comoriens.* Paris: CILF, 1980.

Rouveyran, Jean-Claude et Ahmed Djabiri. *Reflexions sur le Dola N'Kou ou grand mariage comorien.* Tiers-Monde 9(33):95–127, 1968.

Said, Mousa. Mshe Mhaza: la complainte d'Ipvesi Mgondri dit Bungala. *Études Océan Indien* 3:100–110, 1983.

Saleh, Ali. Danses traditionnelles des Comores. *Bulletin des Études africaines de l'INALCO* 1(2):117–122, 1982.

Sans, Michel. Légende des Comores: la mosquée de Tsaouéni. *France Outre-mer* 280:20–21, 1953.

——. Les moilimu, sorciers des Comores. *Encyclopédie mensuelle d'outre-mer* 29:20–22, 1953.

Shepherd, Gillian. M. Two marriage forms in the Comoro Islands: an investigation. *Africa* 47:344–359, 1977.

Sibertin-Blanc, Christiane. *Islam et particularismes africains aux îles Comores.* Mémoire d'ethnologie. Univ. Paris VII, 1975.

Vérin, Pierre. L'introduction de l'Islam aux îles Comores selon les traditons orales. *Paideuma, Mitteilungen zur Kulturkunde* 28:193–199, 1982.

Youssouf, Said. *Mayotte, légendes et histoires drôles.* La Réunion: UDIR, 1986.

ABOUT THE AUTHORS

MARTIN OTTENHEIMER (B.S. Rensselaer Polytechnic Institute; M.A. Tulane University; Ph.D. Tulane University) is a Professor of Anthropology in the Department of Sociology, Anthropology and Social Work at Kansas State University. An expert on marriage patterns, religious systems, and seafaring traditions, he has conducted field research into the history, culture, and languages of the Comoro Islands. His computer program for the analysis of kinship and marriage systems is utilized internationally. Dr. Ottenheimer is a Fellow of the American Anthropological Association, an Associate of Current Anthropology, a member of the African Studies Association, a member of the Law and Society Asssociation, and current President of the Central States Anthropological Association. His publications include *Marriage in Domoni: Husbands and Wives in an Indian Ocean Community,* published in 1985. He has also published numerous articles in professional journals.

HARRIET OTTENHEIMER (B.A. Bennington College; Ph.D. Tulane University) is a Professor of Anthropology and American Ethnic Studies and the Director of the American Ethnic Studies Program at Kansas State University. She is an expert on African and African-American cultures, focusing her research on music, art, language, and folklore as expressions of ethnicity. She is the review editor for the National Association for Ethnic Studies, a Fellow of the American Anthropological Association, an Associate of Current Anthropology and of the Center for Black Music Research, and a member of the African Studies Association, the Association d'Études Linguistiques Intercultur-elles Africaines, the Society for Ethnomusicology, the Society for Humanistic Anthropology, the Central States Anthropological Society, and the Association of Black

Anthropologists. Dr. Ottenheimer has done fieldwork in New Orleans, rural Louisiana, and the Comoro Islands. She has written and published widely on African and African-American music, language, and culture. Among her works are, *Cousin Joe: Blues from New Orleans* (Chicago), *Music of the Comoro Islands—Domoni* (Smithsonian/Folkways; with Martin Ottenheimer) and a *ShiNzwani-English Dictionary* (SASW).